The Integrated Approach to Student Achievement

2nd Edition

Donyall D. Dickey, Ed.D.

Educational Epiphany
Washington, D.C.

Edited by:
Emily Abrams-Massey, Ed.D.

For related materials, visit our website at:
www.educationalepiphany.com

Copyright © 2017

ISBN – 978-0-9994222-0-5

1750 Pennsylvania Avenue #27066
Washington, D.C. 20038

Table of Contents

Acknowledgements

Just about everywhere I go, teachers and school leaders welcome me into their classrooms, offices, and assemblies and present me with copies of the first edition of this book, for my John Hancock on the title page. Each ask brings me great joy, but has also, for years, caused me great consternation knowing that I needed to pen the second edition this book in light of the shifts in public education and that which I have learned as a veteran principal and district-level leader responsible for the schooling experience of hundreds of thousands of children. But even in the advent of the shifts, the formula for improving student outcomes has not changed. The provision of high-quality instruction that is aligned to the nuanced expectations of the standards, delivered in an environment fully conducive to the process of teaching and learning remains the prescription for America's schools.

So this edition is seasoned by my awesome experience as a veteran principal; Assistant Superintendent and Chief Academic Officer of the nation's eighth largest school district; my experience overhauling the academic program and practices of a large district in the Southeast as Chief Schools Officer and Chief Academic Officer; and my experience as a coach of school leaders, curriculum leaders, assistant superintendents, academic officers, and superintendents over the past decade as the Chief Executive Officer and lead consultant of Educational Epiphany—one of America's leading educational preK-12 consulting firms.

I continue to holdfast to the notion that a quality education is the precursor to a choice-filled life for the children whom we serve as educators. It is our responsibility to ensure that zip code is not a factor of student outcomes. It is our responsibility that the 'least of them' have access to an education that prepares them to compete in the global marketplace. So it is to the teachers and school leaders who chose to teach and lead in communities with complex needs…it is to teachers and school leaders who love their students as if they were their own children…it is to teachers and school leaders who insist that the 'least of them' have access to instruction of the highest quality that I dedicate this book. You make a difference.

I know that you make a difference because public education gave me a choice-filled life. I was one of the 'least of them.'

CHAPTER ONE

Address Low Expectations and Student-Teacher Relationships

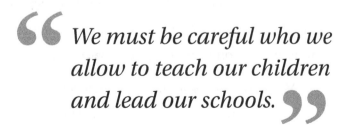

We must be careful who we allow to teach our children and lead our schools.

School is one of the most influential systems in a child's ecology and it is that ecology that almost irrevocably shapes a child's subsequent disposition toward learning and the pursuit of new knowledge. So imagine a child eager to explore, willing to take risks, enthusiastic about engaging his/her peers, and earnestly willing to respond to prompts from teachers, whose schooling experience is constructed day after day, year after year by adults who have made a series uninformed judgments and decisions about his/her intellectual capacity based on race, ethnicity, gender, socio-economic status, family structure, or the zip code in which the neighborhood school resides.

Not one conscientious educator or policy maker reading this book would allow his/her offspring to be knowingly subjected to adults who would, even in the slightest, underserve his/her child for any of the aforementioned reasons. Yet everyday, on our collective watch, children are met as they step off the school bus onto campus, as they enter the schoolhouse, as they open their lockers, and as they enter their classrooms by adults who harbor low expectations for the same children whom they have taken a pledge to serve to the best of their ability. And you know what? Many of our children can sense the low expectations that adults have of them. They often know and can sometimes articulate how adults with low expectations make them feel, but are we listening? Equally disconcerting is the fact that many of our children do not have a mechanism for processing or confronting the intangible, low expectations that they are subjected to each day, so as a result, they turn inward, they disengage, they fail to be available emotionally to receive the education that they deserve and inadvertently their consequent behavior reinforces the stereotypes projected upon them by the adults who should have known better than to judge books by their covers.

My scholarly research and experience as a teacher and school administrator (at the elementary, middle, and high school level) has shown me, without fail, that outside of expert-level knowledge of the content and effective delivery of instruction, the greatest catalysts of improvements in academic outcomes is a student-teacher relationship characterized by care, mutual respect, and high expectations. After all, the unit of change for student achievement and school improvement is not central office; it's not a new textbook or basal reader; and it's not even a new set of state-wide curricular standards. The unit of change for student achievement and school improvement is the classroom.

Wanting to better understand the impact of student-teacher relationships and teacher expectations on student achievement, I extensively interviewed eight African American middle school boys in a high-poverty, urban middle school in the Northeast. Each pupil reported the existence of a strong relationship between respectful interactions, high expectations, and their demonstrated ability to achieve academically. Without reluctance, the boys explicitly stated that it was their teachers who had the greatest effect on their desire and subsequent ability to achieve academically. Anthony and Andrew were specific about how their teachers motivated them to achieve academically. They described the motivating force as teachers' concern for them as students. Anthony stated,

"The teachers care about your learning. They want you to get it. I know the teachers and they know me. They make me pay attention. They get on me [when I don't]. They tell me to stay focused and pay attention."

Andrew argued vehemently,

"They give you a chance to do better…to hand in your work even if you are absent. They care. They make sure that you know what you need to know and need to have in your head. And even if the work is hard, they tell you that you can do it if you try."

When asked to identify and discuss that which has the greatest influence on his desire to achieve, Earnest said without hesitation, "It's the teachers. They make you want to learn." Harold responded similarly, "The teachers make me want to achieve. They care about your attendance." When asked how the adults in their classrooms regarded them, the boys overwhelmingly described their teachers' treatment of them with one phrase—"With respect." The boys also argued that the respect they are shown held them accountable for their behaviors and academic performance and subsequently required them to interact with the teachers in a comparable fashion. Anthony said,

"The teachers treat me with respect. That makes me want to allow them to teach what they have to teach. The respect that they show me requires me to do their work. It makes me want to hear what they have to say and teach. If I ruin the respectful relationship, the teacher will care less."

On the same accord, Keith said,

"The teachers treat me with respect. If I am doing something wrong, they tell me. Then I will straighten up. They take me to the side to correct me. They don't put me on the spot to embarrass me. That helps me to get back on track and keep on learning. It makes me want to show respect back by learning and not talking or interrupting."

Charles agreed saying,

"The teachers are respectful. They don't say bad stuff to me. They tell me 'good job' when I do well and if I am acting up, they correct me, which makes me want to learn from my mistakes and do well in school."

Daniel offered this quote to explain how a caring, respectful, teacher with high expectations translates into willingness to learn, "They treat me with respect and fairness. No racism or difference in how boys and girls are treated. Since they don't take sides, I can learn from them and participate in class." When describing how his relationships with teachers influence his desire to achieve academically, Harold said, "They are nice and welcoming. They say good morning and good to see you. They even hug you. And because I look up to them, that makes me want to come to school everyday and learn more." Earnest responded similarly, saying, "They treat me well and it impacts my grades because they treat me so well that it makes me want to achieve." Lastly, Andrew stated, "The teachers have manners. They don't do bad things to students. When they [the teachers] treat you well and believe in you, it makes you think that you can do well on a test."

In short, the middle school boys with whom I spoke, overwhelmingly linked student-teacher relationships and high teacher expectations to their willingness and capacity to achieve academically. They reported that because teachers were caring, respectful and believed in their intellectual capacity to achieve, it became incumbent upon them to: (a) respond in-kind by engaging in instruction authentically; (b) refrain from engaging in disruptive behaviors; and (c) demonstrate the acquisition of new knowledge and skills whether through classwork, homework, or performance on quizzes and tests. The boys also regarded the constant reminders to focus and remain focused as useful and reflective of their teachers' concern for their wellbeing. Equally significant is the notion suggested by the boys that their teachers' high classroom expectations transferred to expectations in non-classroom settings reinforcing the importance of exercising executive functioning to maximize access to instructional time. Lastly, the boys described a link between the quality and rigor of classwork and homework and high teacher expectations. The boys purported that their classwork and homework assignments supported their abilities to perform academically, think critically, and problem solve as opposed to regurgitate information in the same form it was presented by the teacher. They believed that access to this level of instruction was directly connected to their teachers' belief in their intellectual capacity to do the work, which fueled their engagement and drive to achieve.

Low expectations are just as damaging to student achievement and school improvement as high expectations are helpful. Low teacher expectations are manifested through: (a) poor planning, (b) instruction characterized by rote memory tasks or activities that require students to regurgitate information in the same form in which it was disseminated by the teacher; and (c) an absence of routine, reflective practices that require the use of post-instruction student outcome data to drive subsequent instructional decisions, including re-teaching opportunities and flexible grouping (even in secondary classrooms where teacher directed centers are often overlooked as a strategy for closing the achievement gap).

Low expectations, as expressed through poor planning, are made evident by an absence of and in some cases a teacher's reluctance to compose a lesson progression that includes a 3–7 day outline of instruction linked to a standard that we know will be assessed with attention to a performance-based objective; a plan for teaching and assessing student knowledge of general and domain specific vocabulary; and strategically selected instructional materials necessary to facilitate the gradual release process and multiple formative assessments. How can one facilitate sound, thoughtful instruction without a plan? It is widely known that a student taught by an ineffective teacher for one year (in any content area) needs two consecutive years of sound instruction soon thereafter in order to regain lost ground. It is also widely known that a student instructed by an ineffective teacher for two consecutive years never recovers in that content area. Our children cannot afford to be subject to haphazard instruction. Far too much is at stake. There are too many different ability levels and knowledge gaps in our classrooms and those differences must be addressed by a solid lesson plan. In fact, teaching without a lesson plan is equivalent to driving from coast to coast without a roadmap; you might get to your destination eventually, but not without a significant number needless wrong turns.

Without a lesson plan, how does one...

- Make formal considerations for materials of instruction,

- Strategically link prior learning to new learning opportunities,

- Introduce unfamiliar words and concepts in the content to be taught,

- Model skills to be acquired,

- Place formative assessments strategically throughout the lesson (including cooperative practice opportunities, which allows for peer coaching), and...

- Formulate independent assessments, which are to be used to drive subsequent instructional decisions?

I earnestly believe that if we, as teachers and school leaders, insisted that teaching in our classrooms and schools were representative of the quality of instruction that we require for our own children each day, that previously underperforming children would have little or no difficulty demonstrating mastery of grade level content and beyond. Scoring proficient on an end-of-grade or end-of-course assessment in English/Language Arts, mathematics, science, or social studies should not be as complicated and difficult as it has become. Students are not failing high-stakes, standard-based assessments because they do not have the capacity. Rather, they are failing, in large part, because they have not been exposed to standards-based instruction. These assessments represent the bottom of the instructional bucket. I have seen it with my own eyes across the nation. Our children aren't being exposed to instruction aligned to the standards. The solution is finite. We must carefully examine instructional expectations set by teacher lesson plans/lesson progressions. School administrators, this is your responsibility. You must not abdicate this responsibility to an assistant principal or to teacher leaders. Likewise school administrators, you must get ahead of the instruction in your building before children consume it. If the majority of your feedback to teachers is delivered post-instruction, you're too late. You have missed the train and children may have already consumed instruction misaligned with the standards.

Student achievement is simple. It is a matter of input and output. The work that teachers and administrators do or don't do at the planning table will invariably determine the extent to which students are able to demonstrate mastery. If students are taught content/concepts to mastery by teachers who strategically plan and deliver instruction aligned to the standards and by teachers who believe in their ability to achieve, the children whom we thought could not achieve at high levels, will not only meet our expectations, they will exceed them. My next point may sound radical and may be contradictory to some schools of thought, but for the sake of the children who: (a) sit in classrooms day after day and year after year and receive poor instruction; (b) enter middle school reading two or three grade-levels below their grade-level expectations; or (c) enter high school reading at the sixth-grade level (which is common for poor and minority students in this nation), I am compelled to make this statement without repentance. Here goes. Permitting educators on our watch to facilitate instruction without a lesson plan is tantamount to malpractice.

The delivery of instruction characterized by rote memory tasks was common 30 years ago and widely regarded as acceptable, but the world has shifted and so must the instruction that our children receive if they are to compete in an evolving, global society. Memorizing content-related facts certainly has its place in the classroom, but that isn't enough. Students should know basic facts about science, history, English (rules for grammar, mechanics and syntax). And yes, students must demonstrate mastery of low-level mathematical concepts and demonstrate procedural fluency of simple tasks, but basic understanding of mathematical concepts is insufficient– conceptual understanding this the new gold standard. Instruction that merely requires students to regurgitate facts without also requiring students to: (a) apply that knowledge; (b) analyze (take apart) content, concepts, or assertions; (c) synthesize (put back together in a new way) content, concepts or assertions; (d) evaluate (make judgments) content, concepts, or assertions; and (e) creating new knowledge and understandings of content, concepts, and assertions, I would vehemently argue is not instructional at all. I would argue that it falls profoundly short of that which our students (regardless of race, ethnicity, socio-economic status, limited English proficiency, and disability) deserve and taxpayers should be able to expect from our schools.

So let's define high expectations. Perhaps the issue is that we have so many different definitions of high expectations that we don't know what we mean when we say we have them. I define high expectations as an unrelenting belief in students' capacity to acquire new knowledge and skills as a result of exposure to instruction of the highest quality. Inherent in the definition is both a belief in the capacity of our students as well as a belief that it is our chief responsibility as teachers to provide our students with access to instruction of the highest quality. When the two aforementioned beliefs intersect, then and only then do high expectations in our classrooms repeal and replace low expectations. After all, the unit of change of student achievement and school improvement is the classroom. It's not central office and it's not the board of education.

The second belief—that it is our chief responsibility as teachers to ensure that our students have access to instruction of the highest quality—is about us as educators and the necessity of taking a customer service approach to teaching and learning, rather than a 'I taught it, but they [the students] didn't learn it' approach to teaching and learning. Students who attend our schools are our customers and consumers of the instruction that we provide. They are the consumers of the schooling experience that we construct and offer to them each day, presumably as if it is the best that we can offer. But is the presentation that we place in front of them each day the best that we can provide? If it is not, then we are complicit in fostering an environment laden with low expectations. Sure, some students enter our schools each day with knowledge deficits and negative attitudes toward schooling; however, our responsibility remains constant...to believe in their innate ability to achieve and to hold a mirror up to our own attitudes and behaviors to guarantee that we remain focused on making the main thing the main thing.

And what is the main thing? It is the provision of standard-based, rigorous instruction aligned to the nuanced expectations of the standards that results in a demonstration of mastery and transfer. Instruction bereft of rigor is the adversary of student achievement and school improvement. To the contrary, instruction that is born out of high expectations is instruction that strategically guarantees opportunities for students to grapple with content and concepts for the purpose of building their individual capacity to think critically, solve problems, and perhaps contribute to what is accepted as knowledge.

So how do we ensure that our customers are the beneficiaries of rigorous, standards-based instruction, underpinned by a customer service model that insists upon high expectations for students and self-imposed adult expectations? My next assertion may sound a bit discordant, but I have to be true to what I have seen in schools as a teacher, leader, and senior district officer of large urban districts. Some people should never be allowed to teach our children or lead our schools. Teaching our children and leading schools requires more than passion. It requires more than a love for children and a desire to impact their academic and social development. Teachers must possess expert-level knowledge of the content and they must know how to deliver that content in a manner that promotes mastery for all children regardless of the condition that they are in (academically and socially) when they enter our classrooms. School leaders must know content as well. Teachers have very little respect for school leaders who do not lead instructionally and they should. School leaders should have an unrelenting focus in the content and student access to the content. Likewise, it has long been 'time out' for school leaders who make harmful declarations to teachers like, "I may not know your content, but I know good instruction." Teachers deserve to be led by school leaders who can assist them in the development of both their knowledge of the content and their individual ability to plan instruction that mitigates the achievement gap. The variety of instruction that closes the achievement gap is instruction that is labored over, critiqued, regularly appraised, and carefully crafted—even co-crafted by teachers and school leaders. If we are to provide children with access to instruction of the utmost quality, both teachers and school leaders must make the paradigm shift and become what Elliott Eisner coined in 1979—connoisseurs of curriculum and instruction.

Teachers as connoisseurs of curriculum and instruction consistently place the mirror of individual reflection in front of their attitudes, behaviors, daily instruction, and pedagogy (practice). They ask themselves the following questions about their instruction:

- To what extent is my instruction linked to a worthwhile content standard?

- To what extent does my instruction require students to ascend the pyramid of cognitive demand?

- What academic language must be taught to mastery in order to ensure conceptual understanding of the content/concept(s) and what is my plan for teaching and assessing students' knowledge of that academic language?

- What is my plan for gradually releasing students from dependence upon my knowledge of the content/concept(s) to independent thinking and problem solving relative to the content/concept(s) under study? How do I use the gradual release process to formatively assess student knowledge of the content/concept(s) under study?

- Did I clear up misconceptions related to the content/concept(s) that could be an impediment to student acquisition of new skills/knowledge?

- To what extent, if any, was my approach to delivering instruction an impediment to or a catalyst for student acquisition of new skills and/or knowledge?

- Do I need to re-teach the content/concept(s)?

- If I do need to re-teach content/concepts, what is my plan for flexible grouping and teacher-directed centers/small group instruction to close the achievement gap?

I have found that teachers who do not reflect on their practice are teachers who are likely to be more concerned with covering the content (getting through the curriculum) versus ensuring that students fully understand the content (mastery). I am of the opinion that goal of teaching and learning should always be mastery and transfer.

Since the classroom is the unit of change for student achievement and school improvement, I have a firm appreciation for Lisa Delpit's assertion that low expectations are a deadly fog formed when the cold mist of bias and ignorance meets the warm, vital reality of children of color in many of our schools. I agree with her claim, however I believe that it is incomplete. I would extend her assertion by arguing that low expectations are more like carbon monoxide—an invisible, largely silent and toxic threat to the academic success of not only children of color, but also an ever-present threat to the academic success of children reared in low-income households, those who receive special education services, students learning English as a second language, as well as students who are underrepresented by their parents and guardians. Everyday, across this nation, academic expectations are set for children based upon their zip code, their appearance, and preconceived notions. This practice is immoral and it has a lasting deleterious impact on both the quantity and quality of instruction that far too many children receive over the course of their prek-12 academic career in America's schools.

So, let us be genuine; few will stand in the faculty meeting to voluntarily expose themselves as one who harbors low expectations for certain groups of students. Furthermore, few will argue against the value of developing affirmative relationships with their students. It will not happen that way. However, conversations in the teachers' lounge, team meetings, and parking lot can give great insight to this silent threat to student achievement and school improvement called low expectations. School leaders and teacher leaders must be responsive to these conversations for the expressed purpose of addressing the harmful behaviors that are the progeny of such biases. In fact, schools that are designated as "failing" by the state's standard already have enough naysayers and sideline critics who do not have a clue how hard some teachers and administrators are working in such a school to "turn it around." What a school community under this tumultuous pressure does not need are people on the staff who, themselves, doubt the ability of the students to perform on grade level or beyond. As the old adage says, "A house divided against itself cannot stand."

Low teacher expectations are a pervasive issue facing low performing schools grappling with underachievement, as well as high performing schools (in the aggregate) with groups of underachieving students. Low expectations must therefore be confronted directly by the instructional leader (principal) and addressed by each member of the site-based administrative team, including the assistant principal(s)—who could with a moment's notice become a principal, department chairs (content leaders), and grade level team leaders at the elementary and middle school levels. Low expectations have no residence in a learning community committed to establishing a culture of instruction that, by design, is intended to be fully conducive to the process of successful, reflective teaching and enduring learning. It will require collective efficacy (perceptions of teachers and school leaders in a school that the efforts of the faculty and staff, as a whole, will have a positive effect on students and that such efficacy can be more important than socioeconomic status in explaining a school's achievement level) to close the achievement gaps and improve our schools in this era. It will take an all hands on deck approach in philosophy and practice.

As you will see in the chapters to follow, the Integrated Approach to Student Achievement is built on the premise and precept that all students, regardless of race, ethnicity, socioeconomic status, English language proficiency, and disability can and will perform at levels beyond common expectations when exposed consistently to high-quality, targeted instruction planned and delivered by teachers who genuinely believe in students' innate ability to achieve.

Table 1.1 and 1.2 may prove useful in your effort to discuss, identify, and develop a concrete strategy for addressing low expectations, subsequently replacing them with high expectations, and building positive adult-student relationships. I recommend that school-based teams engage in this discussion with attention to evidence of low expectations by adult group in your building, not to spur animosity between and among personnel groups, rather to deliberately address low expectations and the perception of low expectations head on. Student achievement depends upon it.

Table 1.1—Resetting Expectations Action Planning Template

Evidence/Perception of Low Expectations Demonstrated by **Administrators**	Correlate Action Step(s)	Measureable Outcome(s)
Evidence/Perception of Low Expectations Demonstrated by **Teachers**	Correlate Action Step(s)	Measureable Outcome(s)
Evidence/Perception of Low Expectations Demonstrated by **Instructional Assistants**	Correlate Action Step(s)	Measureable Outcome(s)
Evidence/Perception of Low Expectations Demonstrated by **Support Staff**	Correlate Action Step(s)	Measureable Outcome(s)

TEACHER NOTE: Use this template with team members to identify the attitudes, beliefs, and behaviors that are counterproductive to student achievement and school improvement that may go under-addressed or unaddressed all together. Formulate action steps for each group represented on the table and strategies for holding members of each group accountable.

Table 1.2—Building Positive Student-Adult Relationships Action Planning Template

Evidence of a Need to Build Positive Relationships with **Administrators**	Correlate Action Step(s)	Measureable Outcome(s)
Evidence of a Need to Build Positive Relationships with **Teachers**	Correlate Action Step(s)	Measureable Outcome(s)
Evidence of a Need to Build Positive Relationships with **Instructional Assistants**	Correlate Action Step(s)	Measureable Outcome(s)
Evidence of a Need to Build Positive Relationships with **Support Staff**	Correlate Action Step(s)	Measureable Outcome(s)

 TEACHER NOTE: Use this template with team members to identify the attitudes, beliefs, and behaviors that are counterproductive to promoting positive student-adult relationships that may go under-addressed or unaddressed all together. Formulate action steps for each group represented on the table and strategies for holding members of each group accountable.

CHAPTER TWO

Establish a Culture of Instruction

" *All learning communities have a culture, many articulate meaningful and measurable instructional goals, but few have a culture of instruction.* "

Of which of the following cultural groups are you a member? – American Indian, Jewish, Italian, Polish, African American, Spanish, or Irish? If you are not a member of one of these groups, you undoubtedly are a member some group. We all are. Here's my point... As a member of a cultural group, you are aware of its correlate belief system, even if you choose not to subscribe to it. For example, the mass majority of people of Irish decent practice Catholicism; Italians are likely tell you that their mothers are extremely nurturing; and African Americans almost always refer to close friends of the family as brothers, sisters, or cousins, although they are not related biologically. Members of cultural groups have insider knowledge of norms and taboos unique to the group.

Another example...if I were a Native American, it is very possible that I would have intimate knowledge of the traditions of my people and perhaps I would be extremely knowledgeable of the themes and structures of the stories told by my forefathers. It is also conceivable that I might also have profound knowledge of the history of my people and I would expect others in my community to have similar knowledge and an ability to converse on topics related to shared values, ideas, and practices. Moreover, I would expect the mature members of my community to teach the immature, in an effort to keep valuable traditions and the belief system alive for generations to come.

So why is it then, that when I walk through schools or facilitate professional development workshops and ask teachers, school leaders, and central office personnel to describe their culture of instruction, I get as many different answers as the number of people whom I ask the question? No two people agree on a description of their school-wide/district-wide culture of instruction, yet everyday, children (poor, brown, black, special needs, and English language learners) are blamed for underperforming,—when in most instances, it is the lack of an agreed upon culture of instruction (among the adults) that has a greater impact on underachievement than demographics ever could.

Permit me to pose a few not so rhetorical questions. Answer them in your private time right here in the book, ask your team members to do the same, and then share your responses with other members of your team. In the discrepancies resides the imperative to taking an integrated approach to student achievement.

- What is the culture of instruction in your school/school system?

- What theories (epistemology) underpin your shared practices? Do you have shared practices, irrespective of grade level and content?

- To what extent does your curricula and curricular materials align to your culture of instruction, epistemology, and shared practices?

What systems and structures does your school/school system have in place to hold members of the learning community accountable for providing students with a schooling experience aligned with your culture of instruction, epistemology, and shared practices?

Now, I am not asking you to describe your reading or mathematics intervention; nor am I asking you to describe the textbooks that the team may have hoped would be the panacea for lack luster teaching; nor am not even asking you to recite your school's/district's vision statement. What I am asking however, is what are the theories (body of rules, ideas, principles, and techniques) that underpin pedagogy (the science of teaching and learning) in your school/school district? If you cannot successfully respond to this question, you and your team have a great deal of work to do. It's no fault of your own, but you must own student achievement if you read this book and do not subsequently evaluate your practice. Once we know better, we must do better—immediately.

Peel back the surface of the rhetoric in your school/district relative to instruction, you will be astonished with what you find.

If your school/district has not asked itself this question (What is our culture of instruction?) and your students are meeting with academic success, I fear the following may be taking place (a) your school/district has demographics working in its favor and/or (b) your student body is achieving in spite of your leadership. If your school/district is underachieving, you cannot expect it to become a higher achieving school/district when the members of your culture of instruction (administrators, teachers, and support staff) operate in the absence of a mutually agreed upon set of values, ideas, and practices. Even if your underachieving school/district experiences a relatively precipitous spike in student achievement, such gains will be unsustainable if the more savvy members of the learning community do not teach and integrate new members into the values, beliefs, and behaviors of the school's/district's culture of instruction that have been responsible for its prior success and survival.

In order to establish a culture of instruction conducive to student achievement and school improvement, four major school-wide considerations must be made. The answers to the following culture of instruction consideration questions will serve as the foundation for the formulation of site-based common beliefs, instructional practices, data protocols, and administrative supports vital for building: individual capacity, fostering a culture of collaboration and shared decision-making, and promoting sustained student achievement and school improvement.

See table 2.1 and figure 2.1 to understand what I refer to as the **Four Critical Quadrants of a Successful Culture of Instruction**. Each school/district that I have led to significant improvements in student achievement, I have taken on this journey of self-reflection and practice. It is the intersection of the Four Critical Quadrants that results in immediate and sustained academic achievement for all student groups.

Table 2.1—Four Critical Quadrants of a Successful Culture of Instruction

Quadrant I	Quadrant II
Instructional Theory: What does the extant empirical research (body of literature) in the field suggest are the most effective rules, ideas, principles, and techniques for promoting student achievement? Emphasis should be given to rules, ideas, principles, and techniques that are tested, tried, and true – and meet the gold standard for scientific inquiry relative to: methodology, data collection, instrumentation, population sampling, and acknowledgement of limitations, and researcher bias. All research is not created equally.	**Instructional Imperatives:** What are the school-wide/district-wide instructional practices that promote student achievement and school improvement? • These imperatives should align with the international instructional shifts for English/Language Arts, Social Studies, Science, and the Technical Subjects. • These imperatives should align with the international shifts for Mathematics, the 8 Standards for Mathematical Practice, and 10 Characteristics for a Worthwhile Mathematical Task.
Quadrant III	**Quadrant IV**
Data Analysis: What data points should be collected and by whom? To whom should the data be reported? At what frequency should the data be reported? Through which communication methods should the data be reported? In what settings should the data be reported?	**Administrative Support:** How does the site-based administrative team provide consistent support for teachers and support staff for the purpose of mitigating or removing obstacles to student achievement and school improvement? School improvement is not a spectator sport for school leaders. They should have their sleeves rolled up as active participants in the effort.

Figure 2.1—Four Critical Quadrants of a Successful Culture of Instruction

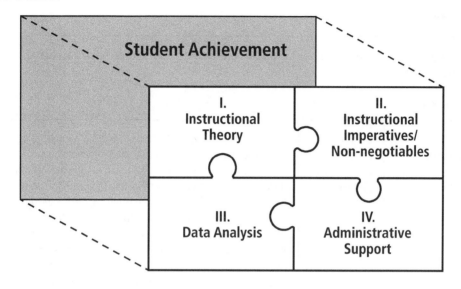

 TEACHER NOTE: The interaction of the four quadrants produces learning communities that are able to lift the tide of instruction for all students, driving actionable, replicable, and measurable improvements in student achievement.

In the next several pages, I will expound upon what I earnestly believe to be sound, gold standard theories based upon empirical research for Quadrant I of the Four Critical Quadrants of a Successful Culture of Instruction. It is upon these theories (Integrated Approach Components) that I suggest schools/districts begin the construction of their improved culture of instruction and their solid foundation for cultivating and sustaining student achievement.

Quadrant I: Instructional Theory

Table 2.2

Theory/Integrated Approach Element	Theorist	Research-Based Description/Findings
Cognitive Pluralism/Higher Order Thinking	Eisner (1979) and Bloom (1956)	Students who are exposed to instruction that requires them to think beyond the memorization and rote learning are exponentially more likely to become critical thinkers with the ability to become problem solvers able to independently ascend the pyramid of cognitive demand (from factual knowledge [regurgitation] to understanding, to application, to analysis [deconstructing ideas and concepts], to synthesis [deconstructing ideas and concepts and putting them back together in a new way], to evaluating [critiquing the reasoning of others], to creating [adding to the what is observed or known]).
Authentic Intellectual Instruction/Work	Newmann, Byrk, and Nagoaka (2001)	Students who are exposed to instruction characterized by challenging intellectual work achieved standardized test scores 20% higher than the national average and outperformed their unexposed peers by as much as 32 points in reading and 48 points in mathematics.
Cooperative Learning and Small Group Instruction	Baker, (1999); Hudley (1997); Quinn (2002)	Students are more likely to demonstrate mastery of content/concepts when they are given access to curriculum-driven opportunities to grapple with content/concepts in accountable learning cohorts characterized by a focus on: (1) peer coaching, (2) standards-based task completion, and (3) skill attainment. Students benefit from participating in flexible, needs-based, small group instruction with the teacher, while their peers who have mastered the content are permitted to engage in extension activities related to the core content. Findings from numerous studies on these strategies suggest that ethnically and linguistically diverse students demonstrate significant academic gains, improved behavior and attendance, self-confidence and motivation, and school and classmates satisfaction when given this opportunity.

Theory/ Integrated Approach Element	Theorist	Research-Based Description/Findings
Co-Teaching	Wilson and Michaels (2006)	The researchers found that all students responded favorably to co-teaching by indicating receiving better grades, developing improved literacy skills, and an interest in participating in co-taught classes in the future. Students with disabilities reported that co-taught classes gave them the opportunity to gain access to the general curriculum and general education students reported that co-taught classes provided them the opportunity to be exposed to higher levels of abstraction, concept development, and skill development.
Guided Notes	Patterson (2005)	When minority and students with disabilities were provided with partially completed notes, they overcame the challenge of simultaneously listening to the teacher lecture, processing information, deciding what is important, and recording important content/concepts to remember.
Teacher Expectations	Fisher (2005)	The researcher found that the majority of teachers within a school had prejudged their underachieving students prior to examining their individual, academic strengths and weaknesses, which invariably impacted student performance in the core content areas.
Gradual Release of Responsibility	Fisher and Frey (2008)	Students are more likely to demonstrate mastery of content/concepts when they have consistent access to explicit instruction that includes: (1) an expert-level teacher model of the skill to be demonstrated by students at the close of a lesson or series of lessons, (2) an opportunity to guide the teacher in order to model their developing understanding of the content/concept(s) [in the large group setting], (3) an opportunity to work in small/groups [preferably in pairs] in order to demonstrate developing mastery of the content/concept(s) while the teacher formatively assesses each group, providing assistance where necessary, and (4) an opportunity to assess individual students' knowledge of the content/concept(s) as a final formative assessment prior to beginning the next unit of study.

In the next several pages, I will make note of and discuss a series of instructional imperatives or non-negotiables that should become, not only a part of teachers' and school leaders' lexicon for the purpose of engaging in professional discourse, professional learning, and reflective practice, but also for the purpose of coming to consensus around that which your community "holds-tight" to in your culture of instruction. This quadrant can make or break your school's/district's ability to drive student achievement—at its core is protecting and guaranteeing the quality of instruction through the alignment of teachers' content knowledge with their use of content language, and content-related tools.

Quadrant II: Instructional Imperatives

1. Expert-Level Knowledge of State Standards

With the exception of the state of Texas, which has adopted the Texas Essential Knowledge and Skills (TEKS), most states have adopted a set of standards for English/Language Arts and Mathematics that, as much as some may not wish to admit, are based on the Common Core State Standards (CCSS). Most states have adopted a unique set of standards for Social Studies informed by their unique state history and Science, most of which are built upon the foundation provided by the Next Generation Science Standards. Lastly, most states have adopted a set of secondary Literacy Standards for Social Studies, Science, and the Technical Subjects, which are being ignored writ large. It's important to note that the state standards, CCSS or TEKS or otherwise are NOT a curriculum—They are a set of carefully constructed standards upon which curricula can be designed. The tripartite imperative is to ensure that teachers and school leaders have a firm understanding of the standards and that a relentless emphasis is placed on: (1) teacher knowledge the standards, (2) the use of academic language aligned to the standards is in the classroom [Why? The language of the standard is the language of the assessment. As long as doors are closed in children's face because of their performance of on a standardized assessment, they must be exposed to the language of the assessment], and (3) the alignment of instructional materials utilized to deliver instruction and to assess students' developing understanding of the standards must be aligned with the demands of the standards.

Unfortunately, what I have just described is not the rule in our nation's schools, rather the exception to the rule. How can we hold children accountable for proficiency on a standards-based assessment at the end of a course or at the end of a school year while we have been guilty of not giving them unobstructed access to standards-based instruction all school year?—Malpractice.

The state standards must be your school's/district's instructional starting point; they identify the skills that will be invariably assessed by grade level and content area. This important document should be utilized to drive instructional decisions. It is the document against which you must judge all other documents, including but not limited to: (1) your district's curriculum [often written by employees who do not fully understand the standards themselves], (2) your interim/quarterly assessments [often purchased from companies whose writers do not fully understand the standards], and (3) curricular materials purchased from vendors who do not fully understand the standards. See the pattern?

2. Expert-Level Knowledge of General and Domain Specific Academic Language

There are a finite number of tier II vocabulary words that students will encounter as they read and perform tasks related to grade-level content. These vocabulary words are typically the same words in prek-grade 2, grades 3-5, grades 6-8, and grades 9-12 (shifting somewhat in complexity between grades 2 and 3, between 5 and 6, and between 8 and 9). For grades 3-5, these essential tier II vocabulary words include, but are not limited to words and phrases such as: citation, textual evidence, main idea, inference, summary, text structure, author's purpose, author's argument, format, medium, claim, reasoning, and ideas, procedures, concepts, identify, determine, analyze, and integrate. Teachers must expose students to a single, operational definition of these vocabulary words so that students can readily transfer their knowledge of them across content areas and grade bands as they read, respond to teacher prompts, take formative assessments, and sit for annual standardized assessments that will undoubtedly use these words.

The approach to teaching these vocabulary words and their definitions must become "transdisciplinary." In order to become transdisciplinary, students must be consistently exposed to instruction that ensures the use of operational definitions that transfer across disciplines (content areas) so that students are able to demonstrate literacy irrespective of discipline. No longer can we use what folks with low expectations refer to as "kid-friendly" language as definitions of these key vocabulary words. "Kid friendly" is often low expectation code for watered-down and misaligned with the standards. I would argue that it is unfriendly to students to refrain from exposing them to the academic language of the standards, knowing well that these words will be used to pose the questions that can subsequently lock them out of proficiency and close doors in their face.

Likewise, teachers must ensure that students have deep conceptual understanding of tier III vocabulary/academic language. Tier III academic language includes words that students will encounter while reading content-specific texts in a specific discipline, such as: metamorphosis, mitosis, and meiosis in a science course; or words such as: emancipation, declaration, egalitarian, and monarch in a social studies course; or words such as: gestalt, impressionism, and panoramic in an art history course. Deep conceptual understanding of tier III words is the bridge to content mastery. To the detriment of student outcomes and in far too many classrooms, instruction on a particular concept begins and ends without students ever being exposed to the words and definitions of the words that comprise the content. How can this be? The predecessor of content mastery is deep conceptual understanding of the academic language of the content—period.

And by the way, asking students to copy the content-related vocabulary words from the back of the textbook is passé and does not build students' deep conceptual understanding of unfamiliar words and phrases. The same is true for asking students to use a vocabulary word in a sentence in order to assess their deep conceptual understanding of a word or phrase. It is also worth adding that vocabulary language development is not about a "word of the day." Often, the only person who cares an iota about the word of the day is the poor soul who is sharing the word of the day via the morning announcements; so help me to help them to save their time and energy. Cease and desist this antiquated practice.

Students do not understand what they have read in chapter because: (1) they did not understand what they read in a paragraph, (2) because they did not understand what they read in a particular sentence, (3) because they did not understand individual words, (4) because they did not understand Latin and Greek word parts (prefixes, root words, and suffixes) as they encounter them in a given or self-selected text. There is no such thing as big tier II or tier III words. Most of them are made up of small word parts that far too many teachers ignore and wonder why students don't acquire conceptual understanding of grade level content. Vocabulary development is about taking advantage of curriculum-driven/in-context opportunities to teach students to make sense of Latin and Greek word parts.

Ninety-seven percent of the words that students will encounter as they read will come from the 30 most commonly used prefixes, 30 most commonly used root words, and the 30 most commonly used suffixes. What is your school's/district's plan for teaching and assessing students' knowledge of these word parts and affixes (prefixes and suffixes)? If you do not have one, you should not expect students to create meaning as they read.

A strategic focus on providing students, grades kindergarten to grade 12, to curriculum-driven opportunities to learn Latin and Greek word parts will invariably build students' vocabulary and ability to create meaning while they read. Many students who appear to have decoding issues, actually have meaning issues. They can decode and pronounce the words they read; however, they are locked out of the meaning of a significant number of words in a given text. Creating meaning as one reads is a prerequisite of ascending the pyramid of cognitive demand. For more information on this element of the Integrated Approach to Student Achievement, see chapter 4.

Refer to the next three pages for a list of the 30 most commonly used prefixes, root words, and suffixes.

Most Commonly Used Prefixes

Prefix—A word part added that can be added to the beginning of a root word or a base word.

anti—against	**auto**—self	**bi**—two
circum—around	**co, con, com**—with	**contra**—against
de—opposite	**dis**—reverse/opposite	**en, em**—to cause
ex—out	**in, im, il, ir**—not	**inter**—between
macro—large	**micro**—small	**mid**—middle
mis—wrongly	**mono**—one	**non**—not
poly—many	**post**—after	**pre**—before
re—back/again	**semi**—partly	**sub**—under
super—above	**syn**—same time	**trans**—across
tri—three	**un**—not	**uni**—one

Most Commonly Used Root Words

Root Word—A word part to which affixes (prefixes and suffixes) may be added to create related words.

audi—hear	**auto**—self	**bene**—good
bio—life	**chrono**—time	**cred**—believe
dict—say	**duc**—lead	**fid**—truth, faith
flex—bend	**gene**—give birth	**geo**—earth
graph—write	**greg**—group	**jur, jus**—law
log—thought	**luc**—light	**man**—hand
mand—order	**mis, mit**—send	**omni**—all
path—feel	**phil**—love	**phon**—sound
photo—light	**port**—carry	**scrib**—write
sens, sent—feel	**spec, spect, spic**—look	**tele**—far off
terr—earth	**vac**—empty	**vid, vis**—see

Most Commonly Suffixes

Suffix—A word part that can be added to the end of a root word or base word.

able, ible—can be done	**acy**—state or quality of	**al**—act or process of
al, ial—pertaining to	**ate**—become	**dom**—place or state of
ed—past tense	**el, er, or**—one who	**en**—become
er—comparative	**ess**—female	**ful, ous**—full of
ic, ical—pertaining to	**ify, fy**—make or become	**ing**—present participle
ion, tion, ation—act, process of	**ish**—somewhat like or near	**ism**—characteristic of
ist—one who	**ity, ty**—quality of	**ize, ise**—make or become
less—without	**ly**—characteristic of	**ment**—act of, result of
ness—state of	**ology**—study, science	**s, es**—more than one, plural
ship—position held	**ward**—in the direction of	**y**—having the quality of

3. Action Plan for English/Language Arts and Mathematics

Develop and implement a plan of action designed to explicitly teach and assess all students' knowledge of a subset of standards-based skills that will be embedded in end-of-grade and/or end-of-course assessments for the tested grades in English/Language Arts and mathematics. The Action Plan is simply a series of 5-question quizzes (short cycle assessments) designed to give teachers and administrators real-time data on 10–15 skills derived from broad standards that we know will be tested on the interim assessments throughout the year and ultimately the end-of-grade and/or end-of-course assessments. The skills that are taught and assessed through the Action Plan must not exceed the grade-level assessment limits. Assessment limits represent the most that will be assessed relative to a given standard and by default, becomes the very least that should be assessed. If an assessment limit exists for a particular standards-based skill, it will be evident in the standard. The table below depicts the process of examining and standard, extracting the skill to be tested through a brief, 5-question short cycle assessment, and identifying the assessment limit where one exists. For more information on this instructional imperative, see chapter 7.

Table 2.3—Action Plan/Short Cycle Assessment/Assessment Limit Examples for English/Language Arts

Grade	Standard	Extracted Skill(s)	Assessment Limit
4	Describe the overall structure (e.g., chronology, comparison, cause/effect, problem/solution) of events, ideas, concepts, or information in a text or part of a text.	Text Structures	6 Text Structures: Sequential, Chronological, Descriptive, Compare/Contrast, Cause/Effect, and Problem/Solution
7	Determine an author's point of view or purpose in a text and analyze how the author distinguishes his or her position from that of others.	Point of View Author's Purpose	Determining author's purpose; Determining author's point of view; Distinguishing author's point of view from that of others
9	Determine a central idea of a text and analyze its development over the course of the text, including how it emerges and is shaped and refined by specific details; provide an objective summary of the text.	Summarizing	Analyzing the development of central idea over the course of the text; Constructing objective summaries

Table 2.4—Action Plan/Short Cycle Assessment/Assessment Limit Examples for Mathematics

Grade	Standard	Extracted Skill(s)	Assessment Limit
6	Write and evaluate numerical expressions involving whole-number exponents.	Expressions	Exponents no greater than 10
7	Decide whether two quantities are in a proportional relationship, e.g. by testing for equivalent ratios in a table or graphing on a coordinate plane and observing whether the graph is a straight line through the origin.	Ratios and Proportional Relationships	Examining the relationship between two quantities; Testing equivalent ratios in a table; Graphing two quantities on a coordinate plane
Alg. 1	Create equations in two or more variables to represent relationships between quantities; graph equations on coordinate axes with labels and scales.	Equations (that describe numbers or relationships)	Creating equations in two or more variables; Graphing on coordinate axes with labels and scales

4. Performance-Based Objectives Linked to State Standards

For optimal results, objectives that inform and drive instruction should be derived from a state standard. Why should objectives be derived from a state standard? Doing so ensures that students who will be assessed on their knowledge of state standards via the end-of-course and/or end-of-grade assessments are actually prepared for the cumulative assessment opportunity all year long—as opposed to the "drop everything and prepare for the test approach" to improving student achievement. Test prep is the default of the amateur school leader. The only test prep that children need is high quality daily instruction. Make sense?

Why would a teacher plan and deliver instruction that is not linked to a standard? I have found several reasons consistently across state lines, grades and content areas: (1) due to no fault of their own, teachers are unfamiliar with the demands of the standards; (2) administrators are unfamiliar with the demands of the standards, therefore it is not a focus of the faculty; (3) teachers and school leaders are unfamiliar with the standards and do not care to become more familiar with them; and (4) the curriculum guides from which teachers are required to teach, are insufficient to build their knowledge of the standards, because they are often written/revised in the summer months by good intentioned employees who, sometimes, do not fully understand the demands of the standards.

Secondly, objectives that inform and drive instruction should be composed in the know and do format. "Know & Do" performance-based objectives are one-part content and one-part higher-order thinking. The "know" portion of the objective should be content knowledge and/or skills that students must have mastery-level knowledge of in order to perform the "do" portion or the higher-order thinking portion of the objective (which should take students up the pyramid of cognitive demand). Performance-based objectives honor your school's/district's curriculum requirements, but also recognize the importance of requiring students to "do something" with that which the knowledge/skills that they have acquired—hence the term "performance-based objectives." Performance-based objectives rid your instructional program of teaching and learning characterized by memorization-driven learning. For more information on this instructional imperative, see chapter 6.

5. Explicit Instruction Lesson Plan Format

To build students' knowledge of the content, while simultaneously building their capacity to use their knowledge of the content to ascend the pyramid of cognitive demand, instruction must be standards-derived, performance-based, and explicit. Unfortunately, all too often, lesson activities fail to meet the "explicit" bar. What do I mean by the "explicit" bar? Let's say the objective for three days is: SWBAT determine the main idea of a text IOT summarize the text distinct of personal opinions and judgments.

[*SWBAT* = *Students will be able to] and [IOT* = *in order to*].

If students are to be able to determine the main idea of a text, then the teacher should model for students the explicit process for identifying the key details of a text and discussing how the collection of the key details led him/her to the determination of the main idea. The teacher should think aloud so that all students can hear him/her: (1) chunk information from the text, (2) distinguish between key details and ancillary details, and (3) synthesize the key details until an arguable main idea emerges. But that's not all. The second portion of the objective states that students must summarize the text distinct of personal opinions and judgments. So what's the imperative for the teacher model? He/she must also model (think aloud) the process of composing a summary (a brief statement that contains the essential ideas of a longer passage) without including personal opinions or judgments. The teacher must provide students access to a "perfect" model/think aloud of: (1) identifying and collecting the essential ideas of the longer passage in order to (2) compose a summary with attention to excluding the writer's personal opinions or judgments on the topic. This completes phase 1 of the gradual release of responsibility.

Next, the teacher must take the next step in the gradual release of responsibility model by allowing the students (as many as possible) to lead him/her in a think-aloud, performing the same task the teacher performed in the think-aloud. This second phase is important, as it allows the teacher to formatively assess students developing understanding of the skills derived from a standard.

Then, if students are ready, it's important for students to have a collaborative opportunity to work in pairs (phase 3) to perform the same standard-derived task—identify the key details in a text in order to determine the main idea and summarize the text distinct of personal opinions and judgments. Why? So that the teacher can float between and among groups to formatively assess students' developing understanding of the skill(s). Pairs are best because students are more likely to share the responsibility of grappling with and completing the task.

Finally, if the informal data collected by the teacher during the collaborative practice (phase 3) suggest that students are ready for independent practice (phase 4), then students should be given an opportunity to perform the same task (identify the key details in a text in order to summarize the text distinct of personal opinions and judgments) in a quiet classroom without any assistance from the teacher or a peer. Without this opportunity, how will the teacher know what each student knows and can do independently?

6. Strategic Re-Teaching

When students have not demonstrated mastery of concepts/content, teachers should re-teach the concepts/content in the absence of unproductive pressure to get through the curriculum guide by a prescribed time set by people who are disconnected from the classroom and the individual needs of the learners. Rather than inch deep and a mile wide, instruction should be a mile deep and an inch wide. So what should a conscientious teacher do to begin the re-teaching process? Determine during which phase of instruction (i.e., the teacher model, guided instruction, collaborative practice, independent practice) students' understanding of the content, concepts, or process began to falter and begin there. If they struggle in any phase, it's possible that the teacher needs to go all the way back to teaching the academic language that makes up the performance-based objective before proceeding with a re-teach of one of the phases.

7. Standards for Writing in Every Lesson

Many students detest writing because it frustrates them, but writing skills are actually among the easiest to improve. But how? Teach children the major forms of writing and the finite number of text structures that are used to compose informational and literary texts.

There are four types of writing that students must master: (1) informative, (2) explanatory, (3) opinion [K–5] or argumentative [6–12] and (4) narrative. Note that I didn't mention the following types of writing: expository, persuasive, or to entertain. They are not referenced in the Common Core State Standards (CCSS) or the Texas Essential Knowledge and Skills (TEKS). Not one time.

Table 2.5—Four Types of Writing [K-12]

Type of Writing	K–5	6–8	9–12
Informative	✖	✖	✖
Explanatory	✖	✖	✖
Opinion	✖		
Argumentative		✖	✖
Narrative	✖	✖	✖

So now that we have established the four types of writing that students must master, what are the finite number of ways in which informational and literary texts are structured that must be attended to when students compose original texts? First, what is a text structure? Text structures are the intentional patterns used by an author to communicate information to the reader or fulfill the purpose for writing. There are informational text structures and literary text structures. How many informational text structures are there? There are six informational text structures in every state with the exception of one state, Texas. There are seven informational text structures in the state of Texas. How many literary text structures are there? There are three literary text structures in every state, including Texas.

Table 2.6— Informational Text Structures (K-12)

	Text Structure	Definition
1	Descriptive	Texts that describe what a person, place, thing, or idea is like
2	Compare/Contrast	Texts that describe how two or more person, places, things, or ideas are alike and/or how they are different
3	Sequential	Texts that present information, events, or steps in the order in which they should occur, could occur, or will occur without the use of time
4	Chronological	Texts that present information presents information according to the progression of time
5	Cause/Effect	Texts that present information regarding a cause in relation a resulting effect
6	Problem/Solution	Texts that present a problem and information about how a problem could be or has been solved
7	*Proposition/Support	Texts that present an idea or suggested action and support for the idea and/or action

* Texas only text structure

Table 2.7— Literary Text Structures by Literary Genre (K-12)

	Text Structure	Elements of the Genre	Special Note
1	Poems	Stanzas and Lines	NA
2	Stories	Exposition, rising action, climax, falling action, resolution/denouement	In Texas, the resolution is referred to as the denouement.
3	Dramas/Plays	Acts, scenes, lines of dialogue	Multiple act plays should not be introduced until grade 6.

Each lesson (keep in mind that most lessons cannot be taught in a single day) should have a writing component embedded in it, through which students must respond to a content-related writing prompt that requires them to compose an original text (informative, explanatory, opinion/argumentative, or narrative) intentionally employing one of the text structures to organize their words/fulfill the purpose for writing noted in table 2.6 or 2.7.

8. Year-Round Accommodations

Be careful to ensure that students with IEPs and 504s are receiving the accommodations as outlined in official, legally binding documents. Students are likely to reject accommodations made by unfamiliar staffers who magically appear on state assessment days to act as scribes, readers, and the like. For example, if a student's IEP states that he/she should have a reader for testing opportunities, that requirement should apply to each testing opportunity throughout the school year (i.e., teacher generated-assessments, interim assessments, state assessments). Without the accommodation, teachers will get a false read on student knowledge and ability. And worse, the accommodation is the student's right—receiving that accommodation once a year is below the standard of service.

9. Meaningful Work for English Language Learners

English language learners can learn the skills to be assessed at their own individual pace. Will they be able to make inferences from developmentally appropriate texts that require a cognitive leap without an ability to read academic English? Perhaps, but math is a universal language and foundational skills for English/Language Arts as identified by your state curriculum can easily be taught to your English Language Learners. Keeping them busy with coloring or ignoring them instructionally because they do not present behavioral concerns is not fair to them. Provide our English language learners with developmentally appropriate, curriculum-driven, academic work and you will be amazed with how many skills they can master in a short period time. In my final principalship, the English Language Learners led the school in gains after one year, exceeding 50% gains in both English/Language Arts and mathematics. How? We simply provided our English language learners with equitable access to standards-based instruction characterized by a focus on academic language and gradual release of responsibility.

10. Use of Manipulatives to Teach Abstract Mathematical Concepts

Students who struggle in mathematics need access to curriculum-driven opportunities to use manipulatives to learn abstract concepts. A mathematics classroom without manipulatives is in danger of failing to promote enduring, conceptual understanding of mathematical concepts. Some students will never master the concept of part to whole relationships, fractions, and decimals in the early grades, without manipulating the little plastic fraction circles or manipulating the rainbow fraction/decimal tiles. And why should they have to? Most schools have supply closets filled with them, collecting dust. Teachers should look for ways incorporate the use of manipulatives in their instruction at the planning table, not as an afterthought. Manipulatives build number sense like no other tool I have seen in 20 years supporting improved student outcomes. Students should not leave our public schools after 13 years of mathematics instruction, innumerate.

11. Bell-to-Bell Instruction

Why are kids instructed by adults to line up and wait for the bell to ring? Particularly when so many students in some of our schools have knowledge and skill gaps...when so many of our students are innumerate...when underrepresented student groups in higher performing schools struggle to reach proficiency. How can we tolerate "free time" in classrooms when the United States penal system uses third grade reading proficiency rates to forecast prison construction needs and projected prison capacity of existing structures? Every instructional moment should be maximized. Too much is at stake.

12. Minimizing Instructional Interruptions

Instructional leaders must protect precious instructional time by:

- Disallowing "all-calls" over the PA system during the school day, except for emergencies;

- Disallowing or limiting room-to-room calls during instructional time;

- Disallowing calls from professional school counselors, teacher leaders, and school administrators into classrooms; and

- Disallowing administrative assistants/main office personnel from interrupting instruction in order to forward lunch money, homework assignments, or physical education uniforms to students who left these items at home.

Why can't professional school counselors, teacher leaders, and school administrators walk down the hallway from their office to retrieve students they need without interrupting teaching and learning for the 20 or so other children who are potentially engaged? These interruptions add up and amount to a significant loss of instructional time. Nothing is more important than protecting instructional time.

13. Hall Passes in First 10 and Last 10 Minutes of Class

Arguably the most crucial instructional moments are the inaugural and final minutes of a class period. For this reason, students should have an authentic emergency in order to receive a hall pass during the introduction of concepts/content and the wrap up of a lesson for the day. It's not enough for the teachers and schools leaders to value critical instructional minutes. We must teach students to value limited instructional time as well. This instructional imperative may be evocative of micromanagement, but we must do everything within our sphere of influence to teach and reinforce the value of critical instructional moments.

Quadrant 3: Data Analysis

1. Meetings with Non-Proficient Performers and Parents

Each student who reads or does mathematics below expectations should meet with the principal and at least one of his/her parents or guardians to: (1) discuss the students' previous year's performance, (2) identify strengths and weaknesses, (3) set academic goals, and (4) provide parent and students with tools they can use together at home to close the knowledge and skills gap (i.e., a workbook that provides students with standards-driven practice opportunities, a blank multiplication tables and a timer for students who lack automaticity with multiplication and/or division). These meetings should be scheduled as early as summer months (after summative assessment data is available) and no later than the last day of the first quarter of the new school year. For students who enroll after the first quarter, I recommend that the meeting be facilitated no later than 30 days after the student is officially enrolled.

2. Coded Seating Charts

Many educators talk about knowing their students, but how many have intimate knowledge of students' performance level on the previous year's mandated, state assessments? I recommend that each classroom should have a coded seating chart that gives the teacher and school leaders information about students reading and mathematics proficiency, as wells as their special education and English learner status. Most states have 4 designations for proficiency in the core content areas, such as: below basic, basic, proficient, and advanced. For example, children who scored below basic would have 1 line underneath their name on the seating chart, while students who are basic would have 2 lines underneath their name, while students who score proficient would have 3 lines underneath their name, and the student who scored advanced would have 4 lines underneath their name. A student with specials needs would have a period following their name, and a student who speaks English as a second language would have an asterisk following their name. Imagine the implications of teachers and school leaders being ever cognizant of student outcome. Integrating coded seating charts into your culture of instruction is a simple practice, but I guarantee you they will pay huge dividends.

3. Pre-Tests and Post-Tests

The standard-related skills that will be tested in state designated grades at the elementary, middle, and high school level should be taught and assessed throughout the school year. Students' should be exposed to a number of the skills that reside in the complex English/Language Arts and Mathematics standards beyond the garden variety exposure provided by the district's scope and sequence/instructional blueprints. Every week or two, students should take brief, 5-question pre-test on a carefully selected skill to ensure that they have the requisite skills to engage in more complex standards-based tasks. When students do not demonstrate mastery via performance on the pre-test, they should receive a few minutes of instruction on the skill at the top of class to fill their gaps, followed by a post-test at the close of the week or two week period to measure progress. Why five questions? Students do not need to be over-tested. It does not take twenty questions to determine whether students have mastered a concept. For more information on this instructional imperative, see chapter 7.

4. Data Centers in Each Classroom

Students should be bombarded with their own outcome data. To that end, I recommend that each classroom have a designated data center, which depicts individual and group outcome data. Students should visit that data center on a regular basis to get information about their progress in the weekly or bi-weekly pre-tests and post-tests (short cycle assessments) and other relevant student outcome data.

Because of the Family Education Rights and Privacy Act (FERPA), refrain from using student names on date displays. Instead, consider using student identification numbers to post initial scores and student progress data. Students who are aware or their progress on standard-related skills are likely to hold attitudes and engage in behavior that supports skill attainment. For some students, their experience with success on the weekly or bi-weekly short cycle assessments may be their first and only experience with academic success. Once they experience success, they will want the experience over and over again. For more information on this instructional imperative, see chapter 7.

5. Monthly Reporting of Pre-Test and Post-Test Data

Once a month, after teaching and assessing 2–4 standards-related skills, the grade level team leader (for elementary schools) or the content area leader/department chair (middle and high schools) should report the gains made by students in the grade level meeting or in the departmental meeting. Why report the data? It is important celebrate small victories and to continuously set and reset the imperative for action. The members of the team need to be aware of their individual and collective impact on student outcomes as the year progresses. End-of-course and end-of-year data is autopsy data. The school year is over. It's too late. Real-time data on English/Language Arts and Mathematics data in one-week or two-week intervals represents data that teachers and school leaders can use to make remediation-related decisions (i.e., regrouping, before school/during/after school tutorial, small group instruction, parent communication).

6. Progress Reports

Although your school system may only require an all-subjects progress report every five weeks, under this approach, I recommend that parents receive a progress report every two and one-half weeks. Doing so helps to hold students accountable for engaging the entire marking period, rather than days before they know the five-week progress report is headed to their parents attention. And parents love it too.

7. Needs-Specific Seminar Courses

Students who have an identified deficit in English/Language Arts and/or Mathematics should have an opportunity to register for a quarterly seminar taught by a highly skilled, highly motivated teacher so that skill deficits can be back-filled. Students who are proficient or better on the previous year's administration of the state exams in the aforementioned content areas should be exempt from such a class and should be permitted to select an interest-based seminar on the subject of their choice or elective. School leaders, make absolutely certain that English/Language Arts and Mathematics seminar teachers have high quality teacher materials aligned to the nuanced expectations of the standards in order to teach the content to mastery.

8. Item Analyses

By content area, teachers should review student responses on district required, quarterly assessments (interim assessments) in English/Language Arts, Mathematics, Science, and Social Studies to identify trends and outliers in student outcomes and responses. Teams of teachers should then be responsible for using data from commonly missed questions to make instructional decisions for re-teaching and flexible grouping. Quarterly, administrators should use the same data to drive decisions related to individual and group (i.e., departmental, grade-level) professional development. Item analyses must be facilitated as soon as humanly possible. Waiting weeks after the formative, quarterly assessments have been administered to conduct the analyses is far too late and will have diminishing returns.

Quadrant 4: Administrative Support

1. Professional Development Series

In order to build faculty and staff knowledge of each of the four quadrants of the Integrated Approach to Student Achievement, it will be necessary to construct a year-long professional development plan facilitated by experts, site-based instructional leaders, teacher leaders, and/or central office personnel assigned to support schools.

Since time for professional development is extremely limited, make every effort to use:

- allocated faculty meeting time to run concurrent sessions;
- during-school administrative planning time;
- full-day, district-wide professional development days;
- interdisciplinary professional learning community time;
- early dismissal days; and
- after-school time.

2. Meaningful and Timely Informal Feedback

Each qualified observer should be responsible for informally observing teachers under their supervision multiple times each week and providing written feedback aligned with the quadrants and elements of the Integrated Approach to Student Achievement. What will make the feedback meaningful? The feedback/accountable talk aligned to: (1) the educational theories that underpin your school's/district's developing culture of instruction, (2) the instructional imperatives/non-negotiables outlined in this chapter, as well as (3) the data analysis/progress monitoring routines recommended in this chapter. You will need to refine your current informal observation tool or develop a new informal observation tool that aligns with the quadrants and elements of the Integrated Approach to Student Achievement that you plan to monitor. School leaders, if you do not put feedback in writing, then change is not important to you.

What do I mean by timely feedback? Either before you leave the classroom, as you leave the classroom, or moments after leaving the classroom, teachers should have access to your meaningful, Integrated Approach-aligned feedback. How do you make this practice actionable? Digitize your feedback using a Google tool so that teachers receive it automatically; or use a duplicate feedback form and simply leave a copy of it on the teachers' desk when you leave (turned face down); or email your feedback while you are in the classroom. School leaders, after you walk out of that classroom one-thousand other important tasks will claim your attention and your good intentions relative to providing meaningful and timely feedback will remain in the intention phase, never becoming actualized.

3. Co-Planning and Co-Teaching with Qualified Observer

This approach requires teachers to submit to an instructional paradigm shift. In order to assist teachers in the transition to providing students with standards-based instruction of the highest quality, it will be useful to teachers to co-plan performance-based objectives and explicit instruction with the support of a qualified observer. This is why school administrators must become connoisseurs of curriculum and instruction, teachers need thought partners who can help them to think through challenges associated with developing their conceptual understanding of the content. They need thought partners who can help them to plan and consistently deliver instruction that does not leave children behind.

This recommendation supports the assertions that school leaders must refrain from verbalizing harmful statements such as, "I am not a math person." If you aren't a math person school leaders, become one. Your students are depending upon you and your ability to strengthen your teachers' capacity and content knowledge. So I hear you say that you have "people" who do this type of work for you. I have two questions for you school leaders, "How is that working for your so far? How are your students performing academically?" If your answer is not 100% proficient or advanced, then you must lead instructionally. The cavalry is not coming; you are the cavalry.

4. Assigning Needs-Based Homework

Homework should be assigned to students based upon their demonstrated "in-class" proficiency relative to the skill being taught. If students struggle during class to summarize a text, should we send them home to summarize more text? Their "in-class" demonstration of proficiency or lack thereof gives teachers real-time data on students' readiness to practice independently. So what does a conscientious teacher assign for homework in the event that students are unable to demonstrate "in-class" proficiency? He/she should assign homework that is one degree in difficulty below the skill being taught and ultimately assessed. See table 2.8 for content-specific examples for making this element of the Integrated Approach to Student Achievement actionable, measureable, and replicable in your school/district.

Table 2.8—Needs-Based Homework for English/Language Arts,

Social Studies, Science, and the Technical Subjects

"In Class Objective"	Homework for Non-Struggling Students	Homework for Struggling Students
SWBAT identify the key details in a text IOT determine the central idea.	Determine the central idea of a given text.	Identify the key (important) details of a given text.
SWBAT multiply and divide whole numbers IOT determine the least and greatest common multiples.	Determine the least and greatest common multiples of given whole numbers.	Complete a multiplication table as fast as you can. Time yourself.
"In Class Objective"	Homework for Non-Struggling Students	Homework for Struggling Students
SWBAT analyze the impact of Christianity on Rome IOT discuss the impact of religion on larger society.	Discuss the impact of Christianity on larger society. Be sure to include in your discussion references to how Christianity impacted Rome.	Identify and list 3 major ways that Christianity impacted Rome.
SWBAT and identify microscopic plant and animal cells and their distinctive parts IOT classify organisms.	Classify organisms by examining their microscopic parts.	Label the parts of animal and plant cells.

5. Grading

Classwork and homework should be graded for accuracy, rather than for effort. Why? That's how the world works. Grading for effort is equivalent to giving every student a first place trophy after competing in the 50-yard dash. As much as we want to promote the social and emotional wellbeing of our students, grading is not one of the areas that we should avoid being transparent with them. It's inauthentic and doing so fails to place a premium on accuracy. Without grading for accuracy, how does the teacher obtain information necessary to drive instructional decisions following a lesson or a series of lessons? Without a grade for accuracy, how do students successfully self-monitor their progress toward a set goal?

6. Homework Bank

A number of students may need additional practice on the skills represented by the pre-tests and post-tests/short cycle assessments outside of during school hours. For that reason, it would be useful to teachers if school leaders procure and organize a set of homework assignments and answer keys for those homework assignments on each of the skills for English/Language Arts and Mathematics. It's a simple recommendation, but teachers will thank you for it.

7. Saturday Academy for Special Needs and English Language Learners

Repetition and practice are critical for the development of skill attainment for students with special needs and English language learners. It will be useful to invite the aforementioned student groups to school on Saturdays for small group instruction in groups not to exceed 5, taught by an expert in English/Language Arts for 90 minutes, followed by 90 minutes for mathematics. After two years of implementation, 71% of my school's special needs population reached proficient or better in English/Language Arts; that was up from 21% proficient or advanced, prior to the implementation of the Integrated Approach to Student Achievement. Similar gains were made in mathematics.

8. Special Education Teachers as Content Experts

Most teachers are in this profession because they are dedicated to the academic development of children. Even with the utmost commitment to children, it is difficult to become an expert on three or more core subjects. Requiring special education teachers to teach multiple subjects will frustrate even the most dedicated teacher and invariably contribute to underperformance among students with special needs. Students with special needs deserve to be taught by teachers who possess mastery-level knowledge of the content. This is why I recommend: (1) inclusion special educators should not teach more than one subject across grade levels and (2) special education teachers assigned to self-contained classrooms should not teach more than two subjects, which will allow teachers an opportunity to attend site-based content meetings and district-wide, content-specific professional development. School leaders, you may need to allocate additional FTEs to make this recommendation actionable, but it will pay enormous dividends if you can pull it off.

9. Para-Educators as Providers of Support in Social Studies and Science Courses

Assigning your instructional assistants to meet the needs of your special education population in social studies and science allows you to build individual capacity of staffers in a limited number of content areas. Special education law does not dictate that students receive support from a certificated special education teacher in social studies or science. Yes, you will have to develop your instructional assistants knowledge of the content, but because they would no longer be required to support students in all 4 core content areas. They would then be available to participate in site-based content meetings and district-wide, content-specific professional development.

10. Teacher Planning Time

Your district's negotiated master agreement has parameters for the use of daily planning time. Know the parameters and make effective and efficient use of the time each week to support approach implementation. Be sure to use one day for teachers to meet to discuss how they plan to introduce the upcoming week's skills of the week as a grade level team (elementary schools) or content area (middle and high schools).

11. Consistent Consequences for Egregious Student Behavior

Once you have implemented this approach, one of the byproducts will be a significant reduction in disruptive student behavior. After all, students will be less frustrated with learning an therefore less likely to act out for the purpose of avoiding academic work. However, with a new, school-wide/district-wide focus on rigor and individual student needs, it will be important to have an agreed upon set of clearly communicated consequences for behavior that represent a disruption to teaching and learning. As a school community, you will need to clearly define teacher-managed behaviors from administrator-managed behaviors. Why? Doing so will: (1) help teachers to calibrate around expectations for conduct, citizenship, and their responsibility for managing behavior in the classroom as a part of their professional responsibilities and (2) assist the members of the school community in the construction of an accountability system around behavioral expectations for students, teachers, parents, and the administration.

CHAPTER THREE

Establish the Imperative for Change with Data

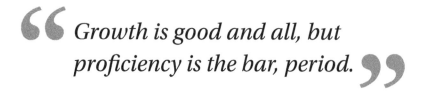

Growth is good and all, but proficiency is the bar, period.

The No Child Left Behind Act of 2001 (NCLB) expanded the federal role in education and quickly became a focal point in education policy and practice. It supported standards-based education reform based on the premise that setting high standards and establishing measurable goals could improve individual outcomes in education or in other words, close the achievement gap. One hundred percent of students in each racial/ethic group and each service group (i.e., students with special needs, English Language Learners, students from economically disadvantaged households) were expected to demonstrate proficiency in English/Language Arts and Mathematics by the close of the 2013–2014 school year. On the surface, the reauthorization of the Elementary and Secondary Education Act (ESEA) appeared to be a winning bi-partisan plan, but it failed to result in the absolute mitigation of the achievement gap and didn't result in unobstructed access to higher quality instruction for all children. Fast forward more than a decade, the Every Student Succeed Act (ESSA), signed into law in 2015, eliminated NCLB's rigid system of Adequate Yearly Progress (AYP) aimed at one hundred percent proficiency in deference to state define goals.

Whether under NCLB or ESSA, the American public education system ought to produce literate and numerate graduates able to think critically, problem solve, and advance our society. We must have systems and structures to standardize the process for evaluating the effectiveness of our schools and the impact of instruction on student achievement. For now, the measure of school effectiveness is student outcomes on state mandated end-of-course and end-of-grade assessments in no more than four content areas: English/Language Arts, Mathematics, Social Studies and Science. Whether we ascribe to or believe in this methodology for measuring of school effectiveness or not, it is our lot as public educators. Each state has four designations that are used to classify student performance in the core content areas – each category speaks to the degree to which students scored below or above expectations on state mandated end-of-course and end-of-grade assessments. Some states use: Below Basic (well below the expectations), Basic (below expectations), Proficient (meeting expectations), and Advanced (exceeding expectations) while other states use other category labels, but they all have the same meaning.

Although the final results from the state mandated end-of-course and end-of-grade assessments are reported in the late summer to early fall of the new school year and are therefore considered autopsy data, these data can be useful to teachers and school leaders to make decisions regarding their instructional program and annual budget. Each member of the school community, including teachers, teacher leaders, site-based & central office-based support staff, parents, partners, and school leaders must become familiar with student outcome data relative to the four core content areas. Data in the aggregate and in the disaggregate should be posted in common areas and meeting spaces as a reminder of the imperative for the evolution of practice and as a reference for context-driven decision making. Before every important instruction-related meeting and content-related professional development opportunity, I would recommend a brief review of relevant data. One would be surprised how doing so can focus participants on that which really matters.

Most school districts require schools to mail finalized end-of-course and end-of-grade assessment data to each home. I support this practice; however, I believe that the practice is only step one of a two-step dialogue with parents/ guardians. You will recall the recommendation that I made in chapter 2 regarding meetings with parents of students who struggled to reach proficiency the previous year in core content areas. In that meeting, it is important to not only discuss their child's end-of-course and/or end-of-grade assessment data, but to discuss the ramifications of continued underperformance. You will also recall that I recommended having students participate in the discussion. Why? So that the student can be aware of his/her performance relative to expectations, share the in the imperative for improving their own performance, set measurable goals, and monitor their own progress against those goals.

Allow me to take the liberty of making an exceptionally clear point about student outcome data and standardized assessments, lest one is left with the impression that I am pro-testing. I am not pro-testing. I am pro-proficiency. If we, as teachers and school leaders, became more familiar with the demands of the standards, we would:

- become exponentially more critical of curricula and potentially deadly "programs" sold to us by vendors,

- be better able to assess the validity/reliability of district-mandated quarterly assessments, which all to often are laden with errors, and

- be better able to protect our schools/districts from taking on new initiatives by "partners" in sheep's clothing.

If we simply sustain a relentless focus on ensuring that our students have access to instruction of the utmost quality, the state tests and subsequent scores that we resent being judged by would take care of themselves.

All to often and to my chagrin, I hear teachers and school leaders boasting of 20-60% proficiency rates in the core content areas as measured by performance on the end-of-course and/or end-of-grade assessments. That's great and all, but proficiency is the bar. Our instruction has to get children over the finish line. If 60% of the tested student population demonstrated proficiency, 40% failed to do so. I do not see an impetus for an all-out celebration. If 20% of the student population demonstrated proficiency, 80% failed to cross the finish line and in most cases, were promoted to the next grade. Yes, I am cognizant of the fact that we teach and lead in the era of public education wherein student growth earns schools/districts points on their school-wide/district-wide state report card.

Students who demonstrate average or above average growth in one school year is noteworthy (considering the academic condition that many of our students are in when we inherit them in our classrooms on day one); however, I believe that far more students would cross the proficiency line if we could simply get standards-based instruction in front of them. If the measure of school effectiveness is performance on a state mandated assessment, then the school-wide and district-wide directive is standards-based instruction for every student. All aboard!

I cannot count the number of classrooms that I walk through as the lead consultant for my firm wherein instruction is in no way, shape, or form aligned to a state standard. It's very difficult to witness. It's even more disconcerting when students are compliant and engaged – all the while being subjected to instruction of lowest quality. It's reprehensible and unfair; then we blame the children for underperformance. Time out.

If you are a public educator, you have undoubtedly seen the Response to Intervention (RTI) pyramid. According to the RTI Action Network, RTI is a multi-tiered approach to the early identification and support of students with learning and behavior needs. The RTI process begins with high-quality instruction and universal screening of all children in the general education classroom. Struggling learners are provided with interventions at increasing levels of intensity to accelerate their rate of learning. These services may be provided by a variety of personnel, including general education teachers, special educators, and specialists. Progress is closely monitored to assess both the learning rate and level of performance of individual students. Educational decisions about the intensity and duration of interventions are based on individual student response to instruction. RTI is designed for use when making decisions in both general education and special education, creating a well-integrated system of instruction and intervention guided by child outcome data.

So how is RTI connected to a dialogue about using data to set the imperative for change at the school level/district level? I have regularly found schools/districts/states with the majority of its students scoring below proficiency excessively focused on intervention programs? Why is this an issue for an instructional leader who understands RTI? If the majority of students are performing below proficiency, then you do not have a pressing tier 2 or tier 3 imperative. You have a tier 1 imperative?

More specifically, if the majority of your students are failing to cross the proficiency line, your instructional program should shift to a focus on the quality of tier 1 instruction that all students receive—to a relentless focus on daily instruction, not interventions. Schools with an upside down population wherein the vast majority of the student body is performing at the below basic (well below expectations) or basic (below expectations) levels, while and a limited number of students are performing at the proficient (meeting expectations) or advanced (exceeding expectations) levels, you have what I refer to as an inverted pyramid and therefore have a an all together different instructional imperative.

If your pyramid is inverted, it is likely your students have been underserved for years. Many of them may even appear to have special needs—but be careful not to over-diagnose. If the majority of students in a classroom, school, district, or state are struggling to reach proficiency, don't blame them—instead, use the data to develop a plan to expose them to the standards-based instruction that the data suggests that they were blatantly deprived of. In schools where the majority of your students are failing to cross the proficiency line, I often hear adults suggest that their students must have unidentified special needs. How can the majority of a population have special needs? That's statistically unlikely. No, they don't have special needs. They have been underserved and under-taught for years and appear to be developmentally delayed when tested, but many of them are not. Teachers and school leaders, you are simply the beneficiary of the cumulative impact of the miseducation of your student body.

If the majority of your student body is failing to cross the proficiency line, then you must reexamine your budget and realign it with your goals relative to student outcomes. Your individual school budget, district budget, or state budget must shift to focus on the provision of standards-based instruction for the majority of your population—(tier 1). It's likely that one or more of the following impediments to student achievement are working against progress:

- Your curriculum is not sufficiently aligned with the state standards,

- Your curriculum is incoherent,

- Your curriculum does not include the actual materials that teachers need to plan instruction aligned to the state standards,

- Daily instruction is not sufficiently aligned with the curriculum,

- Teachers have insufficient knowledge of the content standards and the demands of the standards, and/or

- Formative assessments (teacher-generated and district provided interims) are insufficiently aligned with the standards and do not give teachers and school leaders the predictive data they need to make informed instructional decisions.

If your pyramid is inverted, then you have a slice of your population (tier 2) that has met expectations. So what does this mean for your instructional program? Meeting the needs of students with different ability levels is not a linear process. You cannot ignore proficient level and advanced level performers while you focus on the below basic level and basic level performers. You must meet the needs of all three tiers simultaneously. If you have an inverted pyramid, your instructional program must provide students with curriculum-driven opportunities that challenge them academically and propel them beyond proficiency toward exceeding expectations (advanced status). Lastly, if you have an inverted pyramid, then you have a tiny population of students who have exceeded expectations. So what does that mean for your instructional program? Highly able and gifted students deserved to be challenged academically too. Your instructional program must provide them with curriculum-driven opportunities to extend their understanding of the content and provide them with multiple application opportunities. I recommend project-based learning.

Analyze the Demands of the State Standards and Align Curriculum with Instruction and Assessment

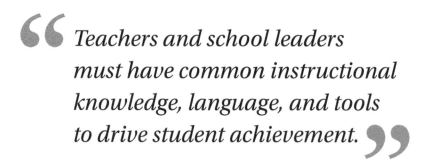 *Teachers and school leaders must have common instructional knowledge, language, and tools to drive student achievement.*

Each state has adopted a set of standards for the core content areas and each year, students in designated grades are tested against those standards. Whether you ascribe to the Common Core, a set of Common Core-like standards, or neither, your state has published a set of informational text standards as well as a set of literary text standards. The standards give school districts in your state, guardrails for the subsequent development of the curriculum. Approximately half of the English/Language Arts standards in your state are informational in nature and the other half are literary. Teachers, teacher leaders, school leaders, principal supervisors, and central office decision-makers (in matters related to curriculum and instruction) must have connoisseur-level knowledge of these standards in order to continuously assess the alignment of the state standards with:

- the curriculum (the scope and sequence or structured guide which teachers are directed to use to plan daily instruction, most often to the letter without, modifications or amendments),

- curricular tools (i.e., materials of instruction such as complex texts, graphic organizers, practice problems, embedded hyperlinks),

- daily instruction (tier 1, tier 2, and tier 3 teaching and learning),

- formative assessments (frequent informal assessments designed to measure the student acquisition of standards-based knowledge and/or skills), and

- summative assessments (cumulative assessments typically given at the close of a series of lessons or unit to assess students' enduring understanding of standards-based knowledge and/or skills).

Why do teachers, teacher leaders, school leaders, principal supervisors, and central office decision-makers (in matters related to curriculum and instruction) need to have connoisseur-level knowledge of the standards with: (1) the curriculum, (2) curricular tools, (3) daily instruction, (4) formative assessments, and (5) summative assessments?—To ensure that students have unfettered access to developmentally appropriate standards-based instruction. If students are to be held accountable to the standards through a state mandated assessment, then the district's curricula must be inextricably aligned with the demands of the state standards Without exception, daily instruction must be aligned with the district's curricula. Without fail, teacher-generated and district administered formative and summative assessments must be replicas of end-of-grade and end-of-course assessments.

There is another reason why teachers, teacher leaders, school leaders, principal supervisors, and central office decision-makers (in matters related to curriculum and instruction) need to have connoisseur-level knowledge of the standards with: (1) the curriculum, (2) curricular tools, (3) daily instruction, (4) formative assessments, and (5) summative assessments. Companies are securing enormous profits on the underperformance of students, schools, districts, and states in the name of "partnerships." They are selling us warmed over curricula and instructional materials that are of minimal use to us in our effort to give students access to standards-based instruction of the highest quality. Moreover, because we do not possess adequate knowledge of the demands of the standards at all levels of the organization, we accept substandard curricula, instructional materials, and assessments and pay a hefty cost—all in the name of improving student achievement. I am not telling you what I have heard. I am telling you what I have witnessed firsthand as an instructionally conscientious teacher, school leader, and senior district-level officer.

Allow me to let you in on the game. Vendors tell our teachers, teacher leaders, school leaders, principal supervisors, and central office decision-makers (in matters related to curriculum and instruction), "We have instructional materials 'aligned' to the standards. They are perfectly 'aligned' and will assist you with improving the 'alignment' of curriculum, with instruction and assessment."

They even make you a deal on the materials as if you aren't aware that the mark up is already embedded in the initial, inflated quote. And we fall for it...hook, line, and sinker. We spend millions of dollars each year for curricula, materials of instruction, and interim assessments that we have to supplement in order to fully align with the standards. Here is the secret. The word 'aligned' is code for something. The word 'aligned' is code for, they are 'a-lying.' Vendors must have connoisseur-level knowledge of the standards to produce and supply curricula, materials of instruction, and interim assessments aligned to the standards. Many of the vendors making a fortune at the expense of our children, simply do not possess expert-level knowledge of the standards– and unfortunately many of them know that they don't have to, because they know that we [teachers, teacher leaders, school leaders, principal supervisors, and central office decision-makers in matters related to curriculum and instruction] don't know enough to challenge them and subsequently decline to purchase their 'perfectly aligned' materials.

So how do you determine the extent to which curricula, materials of instruction, and interim assessments being offered to you are aligned to the standards. There is a two-part analysis that all materials must undergo.

For English/Language Arts, Social Studies, Science, and the Technical Subjects (i.e., art, music, physical education, career & technology, dance, world languages) there is a finite set of pedagogical shifts that must underpin all curricula, instructional materials, and assessments. There is a separate set of pedagogical shifts for mathematics. I will introduce those to you next. As for English/Language Arts, Social Studies, Science, and the Technical Subjects, in order for curricula, instructional materials, and assessments to be aligned, they must be reflective of the following six shifts.

Shifts for English/Language Arts, Social Studies, Science, and the Technical Subjects

Shift #1: Balanced Exposure to Informational and Literary Texts in English/Language Arts

In English/Language Arts blocks/classes, students should be exposed to equal parts informational texts and literary texts. This is a huge shift, both for elementary grades teachers and secondary teachers. Texts in our English/Language Arts blocks/classes have traditionally been significantly limited to literary texts. But to be aligned to the expectations of the state standards, which are about 50% informational and 50% literary, as well as the English/Language Arts portion of the state assessments, instruction must shift to exposure to a balance of informational and literary texts – our curricula, instructional materials, and assessments must make the same shift.

If you don't believe that there is an imperative, randomly select and walk into a random K-8 English/Language Arts block/classroom and ask any student one simple, but telling question, "What are you reading?" Even if they are reading an informational text (i.e., an article, a memoir, an editorial), they will answer your question with these words, "A story." That's right, they have been so overexposed to literary texts, that when they are engaged with an informational text, they call it a story. Even more disconcerting is that teachers do the same.

To be aligned with this shift there is more to which our curricula, instructional materials, and assessments must reflect. The informational texts that we use to teach informational text standards must meet six criteria and the literary texts that we use to teach literary text standards must meet five criteria.

Informational texts used in the English/Language Arts block to teach informational text standards to mastery must:

1. be historical in nature,

2. be scientific in nature,

3. be technical in nature,

4. reflect a variety of eras,

5. reflect a variety of topics, and

6. reflect a variety of perspectives/opinions.

Literary texts used in the English/Language Arts block to teach literary text standards to mastery must:

1. be composed by a variety of authors,

2. represent a variety of themes,

3. reflect each of the three genres of literature: poems, plays/dramas, and stories,

4. reflect each of the three traditions of literature (traditional, classical, and mythological), and

5. reflect a variety of eras of literature.

If your reading/English/language arts curricula, instructional materials, and assessments are not aligned to this shift, then your curricula, instructional materials, and assessments are impediments to student achievement and it's likely that you have been 'a-lied' to by a "partner."

Shift #2: Develop Students' Ability to be Knowledgeable/ Literate in the Disciplines

What does it mean to be knowledgeable or literate in the disciplines? Do you remember your early grades teachers asking you to put on your imaginary thinking cap? When he/she asked you to put on that thinking cap, you thought that you were endowed with superhuman cognitive abilities. You believed that you could do anything. Didn't you? Don't feel bad; I fell for it too.

But your former teachers were on to something. They were actually asking you to prepare your mind to attain optimal success relative to a given task. The same is true for developing students' ability to become knowledgeable or literate in the disciplines. To become knowledgeable or literate in a discipline, one must be able to approach a given, discipline-specific, text as if one is a member of the discipline (content area) from which the text originated. It simply means that, in English/Language Arts classes, that we should be intentional about teaching students to read informational texts like a grammarian and literary texts like a great philosopher; to read historical texts like an historian; to read scientific texts like a scientist; and to read technical texts like experts of the correlate technical subject (i.e., architecture, computer science, dance).

How should this shift play out in our classrooms? Our curricula should prompt teachers to ask students to put on the appropriate discipline-specific reading lenses when they approach a given text. Our curricular materials should support this shift strategically and consistently, and our assessments (i.e., teacher generated, formative, summative/district interims) should move beyond requiring students to respond to one-dimensional comprehension questions (characterized by the lowest level of cognitive demand—remembering) and shift to posing more rigorous questions that assume that students approached content-specific texts as if they were members of the discipline. See table 4.1 for a detailed description of the disciplinary lenses that students should be able to bring with them to reading opportunities across the content areas. I have also defined key terms related to each lens for which teachers must have an operational definition so that common language can be used to engage students in a dialogue relative to this important element of the Integrated Approach to Student Achievement.

Table 4.1—Knowledgeable/Literate in the Disciplines Lenses (K–12)

Discipline	Description of How Members of the Discipline Approach a Text
English/ Language Arts	Students should be taught to approach English/Language Arts texts with attention to syntax, mechanics, and meaning (literal and figurative).
A "do"	The "do" represents that which students are expected to be able to do independently by the close of a lesson or a series of lessons. The "do" portion of an English/Language Arts, Social Studies, Science and the Technical Subjects performance-based objective should always be linked to a literacy skill that we know will be assessed and/or a higher- order thinking skill. • **Syntax**—the rules whereby words or other elements of sentence structure are combined to form grammatical sentences; the way in which words are put together to form phrases, clauses, or sentences • **Mechanics**—the conventions governing the technical aspects of writing, including spelling, punctuation, capitalization, and abbreviations • **Meaning [Literal and Figurative]**—what is intended to be, or actually is, expressed or indicated explicitly (clearly) and what is intended to be, or actually is expressed or indicated implicitly (composed in language that may need to be interpreted by the reader)
Social Studies	Students should be taught to approach historical texts (primary and secondary sources) with attention to bias, credibility, as well as the interaction between ideas, individuals, and events. • **Idea:** a thought, conception, or notion (i.e., democracy, conservatism, racism, sexism, freedom) • **Bias:** prejudice in favor of or against one thing, person, or group compared with another, usually in a way considered to be unfair • **Credibility:** the quality of being trusted and believed in

Discipline	Description of How Members of the Discipline Approach a Text
Science	Students should be taught to approach scientific texts with attention to the relationship between ideas, concepts, and/or procedures; interpreting; analyzing; synthesizing; forming, refuting, and/or confirming hypotheses. • **Idea:** a thought, conception, or notion • **Concept:** an idea of what something is or how it works • **Procedure:** a series of actions that are done in a certain way or order; an established or accepted way of doing something • **Interpret:** to give or provide the meaning of; explain; explicate; elucidate • **Analyze:** to examine methodically by separating into parts and studying their interrelations • **Synthesizing:** to combine (things) in order to make something new/more complex • **Hypothesis:** a supposition or proposed explanation made on the basis of limited evidence as a starting point for further investigation • **Form**—to make; generate; establish • **Confirm**—to establish the truth or correctness of (a statement or theory) previously believed • **Refute**—to prove (a statement or theory) to be wrong or false; disprove
Technical Subjects	Students should be taught to approach technical subjects texts with attention to accuracy, authority, corroboration, and literal (explicit) meaning. • **Accuracy**—the quality or state of being correct or precise • **Authority**—power to influence or command thought, opinion, or behavior (linked to the respect that others have for the speaker/author) • **Corroboration**—to make more certain; substantiate; confirm • **Meaning**—what is intended to be, or actually is, expressed or indicated • **Literal**—related to that which is explicitly or clearly stated

Shift #3: Ensure Exposure to Increasingly Complex Texts for all Content Areas

- What makes the texts that teachers use in your school/district to teach the informational and literary standards for literacy K–12 complex enough?

- How do you measure text complexity in order to ensure that students have access to increasingly complex texts as the school year progresses? What are your criteria for measuring text complexity?

- Are your curriculum writers, who embed texts in your curriculum guide and make recommendations for curriculum-related purchasing aware of the criteria for text complexity?

- Why is text complexity worthy of discussion? What does it ensure? It ensures that students are exposed to curriculum-driven reading opportunities characterized by careful, sustained interpretation of a variety of texts with an emphasis on: (1) the quantitative measure; (2) the qualitative measure; and (3) the reader & task measure.

There are three measures or criteria for text complexity; therefore, texts embedded in your K–12 curricula must meet three criteria in order to align with text complexity requirements and to be 'aligned' to the expectations of your state standards. Number one, texts must be quantitatively appropriate—that is, the Lexile score of the texts that teachers use to teach content/concepts to mastery must be developmentally appropriate. As the school year progresses the texts teachers use to teach content/concepts to mastery must become gradually become more quantitatively complex. As the texts become more quantitatively complex, teachers must be prepared to employ needs-based strategies to build an access bridge to the more complex texts, so that the quantitative complexity does not interfere with students' ability to acquire knowledge of the content and new skills.

Number two, in addition to being quantitatively appropriate, the texts teachers use to teach content/concepts to mastery must meet the qualitative measure of text complexity. Students must have access to texts that expose them to general and discipline specific skills and concepts that include: (1) diverse levels of meaning (i.e., literal, figurative); (2) diverse text structures, including but not limited to sequentially-structured informational texts, chronologically-structured informational texts, descriptively-structured informational texts, compare/contrast-structured texts, cause/effect-structured informational texts, problem/solution-structured informational texts, informative texts, explanatory texts, opinion pieces, argumentative texts, narrative texts including, but not limited to essays, speeches, single and multi-act plays, stories with diverse plot configurations, allegories, and graphic novels; (3) diverse language conventionality (the use of the language to communicate information, including, but not limited to alliteration, refrains, complex sentence structures, rhetorical questions, logical & emotional appeals); and (4) knowledge demands. What do I mean by knowledge demands? A text can become more qualitatively complex for a student if he/she has limited knowledge of the subject of the text. So what is the imperative for ensuring that your curriculum, instructional materials [in this case, texts], and assessments are aligned with this element of text complexity? Allow me to make an illustration.

Do you ever laugh in the movie theatre when others don't? In many cases, you laughed because you got/understood something that went over others' heads. Why? Because in that moment you were able to process a qualitative element of text (movie script) that was intentionally written into the script, by the author, to evoke a response. This is the experience that students need to have consistently; that is, access to texts [for the purpose of performing a standards-related task] that are laden with diverse levels of meaning, diverse structures, diverse language conventionality that require diverse knowledge demands so that they can have opportunities to laugh in the theater too.

Number three, in addition to being quantitatively appropriate, qualitatively complex, the texts that teachers use to teach content/concepts to mastery must meet the reader and task measure of text complexity. For text to be appropriately complex and 'aligned' to the standards, the third measure of text complexity must be met—the reader & task measure. This element of text complexity has built into it a rhetorical question for teachers: What do you know about the reader that you consider before selecting a text to teach a standard to mastery and beyond? Before selecting a text to teach content/concepts to mastery and beyond, an analysis of the students' motivation, knowledge [gaps or lack thereof], and experiences, must be conducted. But be careful here. Do not become guilty of a mistake that I made early in my career as a third grade teacher. This element of text complexity is not a springboard for a soapbox discussion on culturally responsive instruction. This element of text complexity is NOT about the excessive use of interest-based texts. In error, I used texts about sports to motivate my boys to read, but that instructional decision was unfair to them. Why? When they sit for the state mandated assessment opportunity at the end of the school year, they were required to read a variety of texts that were historical, scientific, technical, from diverse eras, on a variety of topics, and from a variety of perspectives in order to demonstrate knowledge of content/concepts. But much of what they read was limited to what they 'liked." So what's the imperative? If students aren't motivated to read texts, teachers need strategies to hook students' interests. Those strategies should be integrated into the curriculum.

This element of text complexity has built into it a second rhetorical question for teachers: To what extent are the texts that you have embedded in the curriculum useful to teach and assess a standards-related skills or concept to mastery and beyond? I was in a classroom some years ago, conducting a classroom walkthrough with a principal and her leadership team as a part my consulting contract, and students were asked by the teacher to determine the main idea of a given paragraph. A customary task, right? Well, the paragraph for which students were tasked with determining its main idea did not have a main idea. Even if the students had a flashlight in the daytime, they would not have found its main idea. The paragraph was made up of disparate, disconnected sentences that did not work together to communicate a single unified idea, notion, or concept. In less complicated terms, the text did not match the task.

So what is the imperative? To what extent does your school's/district's curriculum, curricular tools, daily instruction, formative assessments, and summative assessments 'align' with this shift? Text complexity is not as simple as having classroom libraries. Teachers, teacher leaders, school leaders, and central office decision-makers in matters related to curriculum and instruction, it is high-time to discontinue the practice of permitting vendors tell us that they are selling us solid gold, when they are actually peddling plated gold.

Shift #4: Require Textual Evidence to Support Responses

We have already established that I am not pro-testing; rather I am pro-proficiency. As long as doors are closed in the faces of children based upon their performance on standardized assessments, proficiency on state mandated assessments is a topic worthy of conversation and strategic action. As long as the effectiveness of teachers and schools leaders is based squarely on student performance on standardized assessments, proficiency on state mandated assessments must be addressed by a coordinated effort to provide children with equitable access to instruction of the highest quality—not to the text to support their response, this is a matter of critical importance. Proficiency is at stake. So what is the recommendation for resolving this issue in our schools/districts? You must have a school-wide/district-wide definition for citing textual evidence and hold the team accountable to adhering to the use of it. Students have difficulty citing textual evidence in part, because of the 20–30 definitions they have heard from teachers. Consequently, students are legitimately unsure of which one to use to successfully refer to the text to support a response. By the way, a citation is a quote or reference from a text brought forward as support and citations are more useful when they include the exact location of the textual evidence (i.e., a page number, paragraph number, line number and/or author). The writers of standardized assessments assume that students have been exposed to that operational definition and they construct prompts with that definition in their consciousness. test prep. With mathematics being the exception, ninety-five percent of the questions that children will encounter on state assessments will require them to refer to the text to support their response. What is the imperative? Ninety-five percent of the questions that teachers pose in class to relative to standards-aligned content and concepts should require the same. In order for curricula, instructional materials, teacher-generated formative and summative assessments, and district required interim assessments to be 'aligned' to expectations, the same must be true of the questions embedded in them. Remember, we are not permitting any one to 'a-lie' to us anymore about the alignment of their stock materials to the expectations of our specific state standards.

This requirement has been complicated by the fact teachers, teacher leaders, school leaders, curriculum writers, and central office personnel who support schools do not have an operational definition of citing textual evidence. Why would this be problematic? We have established that ninety-five percent of the questions that children will encounter on state assessments will require them to refer to the text to support their response. But as children go from class to class and grade to grade, they are exposed to discrepant expectations for (1) extracting textual evidence and (2) citing it to support a claim or assertion.

Still not clear? When students go from their English block to their social studies block, to their science block to their technical subjects block, if they are asked to cite textual evidence to support a response to a prompt—and that is a big if—they are met with different expectations/directions for citing textual evidence. Children can easily become instructionally schizophrenic with exposure to so many different expectations around this essential, transdisciplinary literacy skill. This issue cannot persist. It must be resolved in your school/district immediately. Why? If ninety-five percent of the questions that children will encounter on state assessments will require them to refer

Shift #5: Require Writing from Sources

Students must master four types of composition. From table 4.2, it may appear to be five types, but it's actually four. Students are not responsible for opinion and argumentative writing simultaneously. One is a K–5 expectation and the other is a 6–12 expectation. So what's the imperative for curricula, instructional materials, teacher-generated formative assessments, and district required interim assessments if they are going to 'align' to support improvements in student achievement? Teacher procured and district provided materials of instruction and assessment tools must provide students with standards-aligned writing opportunities that 'align' with each of the fours types of composition. What are the four types of composition? When I ask this questions to teachers, teacher leaders, school leaders, curriculum writers and central officer personnel responsible for supporting schools, I get discrepant responses, most of which are erroneous and reflective of days gone by. Inaccurate responses include, "…persuasive texts, entertaining texts, personal narrative." Why is this troubling? Students are supposed to know, so we have to know. One cannot transfer knowledge that one does not posses.

You will recall from chapter 2, the four types of writing for which students are responsible include: (1) informative texts (2) explanatory texts, (3) opinion texts (grades K-5) or argumentative (grades 6-12), and (4) narrative texts.

Table 4.2—Four Types of Writing from Sources (K–12)

Type of Writing	K–5	6–8	9–12
Informative	✖	✖	✖
Explanatory	✖	✖	✖
Opinion	✖		
Argumentative		✖	✖
Narrative	✖	✖	✖

I am compelled to present one final, important caveat about writing from sources. You will note that the word 'sources' in "Require Writing from Sources" is plural. Why? Students must not be permitted to write or speak on a topic(s) from a single source in grades K–12. I'll elaborate. Although kindergarteners may not be able to technically "write" from sources because they may not be independent writers, their teachers can read to them multiple pieces of texts on frogs and require them to speak about frogs. It is insufficient and below the standard of service to permit students to write or speak about a topic as if consulting a single source could ever be all-inclusive on a given topic. Writing from sources is the forerunner of conducting research in later grades. Do not allow children to suppose for a moment that it is acceptable or appropriate to speak or write about a topic after having been exposed to a topic from a single source. At best, their subsequent composition or speech will be uninformed and shortsighted. Set this expectation in the early grades so that is not an issue later.

Shift #6: Include Daily, Curriculum-Driven Opportunities to Make Sense of General and Domain Specific Words

As discussed in chapter 2, there are a finite number of tier II vocabulary words that students will encounter as they read and perform tasks related to grade-level content. For grades 6–8, these essential tier II vocabulary words include, but are not limited to words and phrases such as: citation, textual evidence, central idea, inference, summary, text structure, tone, author's purpose, point of view (perspective), author's argument, format, medium, claim, delineate, evaluate, reasoned judgment, ideas, procedures, concepts, identify, determine, analyze, and integrate. What is the imperative? In order for curricula, instructional materials, teacher-generated formative and summative assessments, and district-required interims to be 'aligned' to the standards, curricula and assessment tools must provide students with access to the same. We have established that teachers must expose students to a single, operational definition of these vocabulary words so that students can readily transfer their knowledge of them across content areas and grade bands as they read, respond to teacher prompts, engage in curriculum-driven dialogue, take formative assessments, and strive for proficiency on annual standardized assessments that will undoubtedly include these words.

We have also established that teachers must ensure that students have enduring, deep conceptual understanding of tier III vocabulary/academic language (words that students will encounter while reading content-specific texts in a specific discipline, such as: anatomical, mitochondria, and gestation in a science course; or words and phrases such as: parliament, judiciary, declaration, and revolutionary in a social studies course; or words such as: onomatopoeia, allegory, or personification in an English/language arts course). Deep conceptual understanding of tier III words is the bridge to content mastery. To the detriment of student outcomes and in far too many classrooms, instruction on a particular concept begins and ends without students ever being exposed to the words and definitions of the words that comprise the content. Our students do not have to continue to have vocabulary deficits. We can resolve this issue straightway.

Why does the average student have difficulty demonstrating proficiency on a basic competency state assessment and why does an above-average student does not always score advanced on a basic competency state assessment? My answers should change the manner in which teachers, teacher leaders, school leaders, curriculum writers, and central office personnel who support schools approach vocabulary development. My answers should also simultaneously mature our ability to be critical of instructional materials that we may have previously regarded as 'aligned' to the standards. Here are my answers...

Students who read/perform below proficiency have an operational vocabulary bank of only 2,500 words, but need one which consists of at least 25,000 words in order to read/demonstrate proficiency. We have to multiply their vocabulary fivefold. But how do teachers teach vocabulary to students averse to reading?

Students do not always understand what the read when the read. Huh? Many students who to appear to be illiterate aren't actually illiterate. They can often successfully read, decode, and pronounce the words they encounter in text—that's what reading is, right? The act of literally reading each word on a page or phonetically decoding words and pronouncing them accurately does not mean that students actually created meaning as they read or understood what the words meant that they read. Still not clear?

Students who appear to be illiterate or who have a low individual, Lexile scores can often read the words on the page, but they don't know what the words literally mean. Still not clear?

Students don't understand what they read in a chapter because they don't understand the words they read in a paragraph, because they don't understand the words they read in a sentence, because they don't understand word parts.

Ninety-seven percent of the words that students encounter in a text, irrespective of content area, originate from the 30 prefixes, 30 root words, and 30 suffixes that I shared in chapter 2. If exposed to, in context, curriculum-driven opportunities to make sense of unfamiliar words and phrases, (1) we will multiply their vocabulary and (2) students will become better able to create meaning as they read—that is, get beyond saying the words on the page to actually understanding the words on the page.

Permit me to raise one practical illustration to wrap up this line of thought. Randomly ask one of your students (middle or high) to give you the meaning of the Latin base word greg-. While you are at it, ask their teacher too see what answer you get... You will be amazed with the responses that you receive. If student must know the definitions of key words parts, as connoisseurs of curriculum instruction, each of us must know as well.

If a student knows the meaning of the Latin root word greg-, and common root words like it, they might have a fighting chance of answering the litany of close-ended vocabulary questions, analogies, and vocabulary-in-context questions commonly found on end-of-course and end-of-grade assessments. The Latin root word greg- means group and gives students a tool to figure of the meaning of so many other words like: egregious (prefix e- meaning out; suffix –ous meaning full of or fully); therefore, egregious, means fully out of the group. Students might also have a fighting chance at determining the meaning of the words: congregate, segregate, aggregate, gregarious, disaggregate and the list goes on. What might we accomplish by simply teaching students to memorize the meaning of key prefixes, root words, and suffixes? We will: (1) multiply their vocabulary, (2) increase the likelihood that they will understand the words they pronounce as they read, and (3) use the knowledge gained from texts to ascend the pyramid of cognitive demand.

Promoting rote memorization is acceptable as it relates to word parts. But where in your school's/district's core curriculum for each subject is this skill strategically and consistently embedded? In which content area(s) are word parts actively and consistently taught to students as a skill necessary for navigating disciplinary literacy? Word parts (root words and affixes) are emphasized in your state curriculum, so you can guarantee that students will be asked questions on standardized assessments to test their knowledge of them, so to refrain from exposing students to these skills is instructionally neglectful and counterproductive to student achievement. Asking students to use a word in a sentence does not result in enduring knowledge of the word's meaning, a student who understands word parts can determine the meaning of just about any multi-syllabic, unfamiliar word.

Table 4.3—Six Crosscutting Shifts for English/Language Arts, Social Studies, Science and Technical Subjects At-a-Glance (K–12)

#	Shift
1	Balanced Exposure to Informational and Literary Texts in English/Language Arts
2	Develop Students' Ability to be Knowledgeable/Literate in the Disciplines
3	Ensure Exposure to Increasingly Complex Texts for all Content Areas
4	Require Textual Evidence to Support Responses
5	Require Writing from Sources
6	Include Daily, Curriculum-Driven Opportunities to Make Sense of General and Domain-Specific Words

*Adapted from EngageNY shifts

Shifts for Mathematics

Shift #1: Focus

Have you ever seen someone speed up to a red light? I can assure you that the first word that came to your mind was not genius. Then why do we drive through the curriculum so fast only to find out that students need more time on task in order to attain mastery and transfer? Some of this rushing is imposed on teachers by teacher leaders and administrators who are being pressured by central office personnel, while others are self-imposing the culture of rushing to get through the content. Either scenario is bad for children. What is the worst that could happen? Students might fail the end-of-course or end-of-grade assessment? If teachers are rushing, students are probably already failing. So do yourself and the children a favor. Slow down and teach the content to mastery and transfer. This shift is about teaching mathematics concepts to mastery over obligatory coverage. It's about teachers significantly narrowing the number of skills and concepts that are taught in a given quarter, semester, or school year in order to: (1) focus deeply on the concepts that are prioritized in the standards and (2) promote deep understanding over algorithmic-driven mathematics instruction.

One final imperative for knowing and doing that may not be evident, that is somewhat hidden behind the name of this shift, is the necessity for facilitating needs-based, flexible groups in K–12 mathematics classrooms. Do you remember your elementary school days when you were a part a small cohort of students in reading? You were in a small group named after an animal like a lion, tiger, or eagle…Fond memories coming back to you?—Sure. But what you did not know then is that your teacher had placed you in an ability-group based upon your performance so that he/she could call you over to that kidney-shaped table to fill your knowledge and skill gaps and/or accelerate your progress. This shift is about: (1) teachers having time and space to teach to mastery and transfer, (2) teachers having expert-level knowledge of the concepts that are prioritized in the standards, (3) teachers delivering instruction characterized by gradual release of responsibility; (4) teachers having intimate knowledge of students' knowledge and skills gaps, and (5) teachers taking a clinical approach to filling students' knowledge and skill gaps through the use of a proven strategy [flexible groups] informed by real-time data. The unit of change for student achievement is and will forever be the classroom. It's where the rubber meets the road. What is the imperative for those who are supporting teachers? Become an advocate of teaching to mastery and transfer and watch the assessments will take care of themselves.

Shift #2: Coherence

Mathematics curricula must be strategically and logically sequenced so that teachers artfully plan and deliver instruction that: (1) connects learning within and across the domains of mathematics [geometry, measurement and data, statistics and probability, numbers and operations in base ten, the number system, number and quantity, operations and algebraic thinking, expressions and equations, algebra, counting and cardinality, numbers and operations—fractions, ratios and proportional relationships, and functions] and (2) connects learning within and across grades so that students can build new understanding onto foundations built through exposure to prior instruction in prior units, in prior semesters, in prior courses, and in prior years. Each mathematical concept cannot and should not be presented to students as a new event, but rather as an extension of previously mastered content. For example, what concept should be introduced immediately following mastery of simplifying expressions? Solving one-step algebraic expressions. Sound simple? I have seen scores of incoherent and circuitous curriculum guides. Believe me.

So what is the imperative for mathematics curricula, instructional materials, teacher-generated assessments, formative assessments, summative assessments, and district-required interims? They must be strategically and methodically designed to promote coherent exposure to concrete and abstract mathematical concepts. Teachers, teacher leaders, school leaders who implement the curriculum and curriculum writers and central office personnel who make decisions about matters related to teaching and learning must have systems and structures that allow for open access to engaging in a bi-directional conversation about the extent to which the curricula, instructional materials, and assessments at their disposal 'align' to this shift. Without the necessary communication structures to allow for critical dialogue, issues with curricular tools persist and languish to the detriment of student achievement and school improvement.

Shift #3: Procedural Fluency

Depending upon the concept and domain of study in mathematics [geometry, measurement and data, statistics and probability, numbers and operations in base ten, the number system, number and quantity, operations and algebraic thinking, expressions and equations, algebra, counting and cardinality, numbers and operations—fractions, ratios and proportional relationships, and functions], there is a finite number of prerequisite skills that students must be able to access and demonstrate with automaticity in order to successfully engage in complex, mathematical problem solving situations. Right? Right. A student struggling to multiply fluently has a procedural fluency gap and will, therefore have significant difficulty with the demonstrating mastery of least and greatest common multiples. Likewise, a student struggling with finding the area of a single triangle has a procedural fluency gap and will, therefore struggle profusely with finding the area of a composite figure. So what is the imperative for mathematics curricula, instructional materials, teacher-generated assessment, formative assessments, summative assessments, and district-required interims? They must provide strategic, standards-aligned, curriculum-driven opportunities to build and assess students' ability to demonstrate speed and accuracy with simple calculations. If curricular materials purchased from "partners" are not aligned to this shift, I am sorry, but you have been "a-lied" to.

Shift 4: Conceptual Understanding

This shift is about providing students with classrooms that value understanding the mathematics they do. I submit to you that one of the most critical antecedents of deep conceptual understanding of any concept, mathematical or otherwise, is deep conceptual understanding of the language of the concept. How can one engage in a dialogue on ratios and proportional relationships without deep conceptual understanding of terms like: ratio, constant, relationship, equation, unit rate, fraction, and proportionality? One cannot. To that end, mathematics curricula must, without exception, give both teachers and students uninhibited access to operational definitions of terms that comprise the language of the concept. But that is only step one.

Teachers must subsequently use the academic language and knowledge of the operational definitions of the concept throughout the gradual release process when they model and think aloud. Likewise, students must be required to use the same academic language and knowledge of the operational definitions when they model for the teacher during guided instruction. And yes, students must be required to use the same academic language and knowledge of the operational definitions when they engage in paired-collaborative practice, all for the purpose of being able to use the academic language and knowledge of the operational definitions to speak and write about mathematics independently. You do know why students need a sentence starter to jumpstart their writing on a given topic? They lack deep conceptual understanding of the academic language. If one possesses deep conceptual understanding of a concept, he/she doesn't need a jumpstart. He/she can self-start.

Beyond the curriculum providing access to the academic language, instructional materials must also provide students with access to academic language: (1) while they work, and (2) where they work, which is why I have written a dozen teacher resource books filled with standards-based graphic organizers with the academic language plastered on the page so that students have uninhibited access to the language while their understanding is under development. We can no longer assume they understand the academic language conceptually. Lastly, teacher-generated formative and summative assessments and district-required interims must use the academic language in the formulation of the questions to which students must respond. There should be no such thing in your school as "drop everything and prepare for the state assessment," students should be in the preparation process everyday.

Shift #5: Application

A proficient mathematician does not need to be promoted to choose an appropriate tool or efficient approach when engaging with a mathematical task in the real world. But we stunt students' proficiency in classrooms when we tell them that must choose a particular tool or set of tools in order to solve a problem. We stunt students' proficiency in classrooms when we tell them that they must use our favorite or go-to approach for solving a given problem. Why? Successful mathematics instruction is mathematics instruction that allows students the latitude to use math and choose the appropriate concept for application without being prompted. What's the worse that could happen? Students will become independent thinkers and problem solvers? Sounds good to me.

This shift also promotes the consistent use of real-world situations as a vehicle for students, at all grade levels, to apply their knowledge of mathematical concepts. What is the implication for practice? Long gone are the days when students are presented with a page full of simple, purpose-disconnected problems—unless of course the teacher is using those simple problems to build procedural fluency. Instead, mathematics instruction in America's schools should have already shifted to instruction characterized by the use of fewer, higher-quality, worthwhile mathematical tasks that require students to cross mathematical domains, making use of multiple skills in order to solve problems that have meaning in their world. Let's shift.

Have your curricula, instructional materials made this shift? It's worth investigating.

Shift #6: Dual Intensity

Which is more important? Doing mathematics or understanding mathematics. The National Council for Teachers of Mathematics and I agree. They are equally important. Our mathematics classrooms should value doing and knowing mathematics with the same degree of intensity. It's great for students to be able to 'get the answer' to a mathematics question and circle it, but it's even better for students to understand the work they did to 'get the answer' and why they did what they did to 'get the answer'—conceptually. You have the pattern by now. You know what I am going to ask next?

What is the imperative for curricula, instructional materials, and teacher-generated assessments, formative assessments, summative assessments, and district-required interim assessments? In order to be 'aligned' with expectations for mathematics, curricular materials must prompt and, in some cases, teach teachers how to make doing and understanding a priority in their mathematics instruction. A dual intensity mathematics classroom is one wherein teachers create practice opportunities for students to participate in "drills" as well as make use of those skills through extended application of math concepts. Lastly, formal and informal assessments must be designed and scored in a way that values doing mathematics and understanding mathematics. A 100% multiple choice/selected response unit assessment can easily fall short of valuing understanding of mathematics. To that end, assessments should require students to respond to open-ended questions, which are more likely to value understanding over the act of getting the right answer.

Table 4.4—6 Shifts for Mathematics At-a-Glance (K–12)

#	Shift
1	Focus
2	Coherence
3	Procedural Fluency
4	Conceptual Understanding
5	Application
6	Dual Intensity

*EngageNY shifts. Although some work has been done to collapse these shifts, it believe that is important to call each of the six shift out before consolidating them.

CHAPTER FIVE

Permanently Unpack the Standards and Provide Tools that Make the Shifts Actionable, Replicable, and Measurable

" *School leaders' expectations for instructional rigor and alignment with the standards ought to match their efforts to provide teachers with the tools they need to get the job done.* "

One of the main aims of rolling out state standards is the provision of instruction of the highest quality, irrespective of a given zip code within a state. The quality of instruction should not vary based on the zip code in which a school building/district resides. With that said, I am a proponent of state level expectations; however, I must argue that standards alone, do not guarantee that students will have access to instruction of highest quality. Because the unit of change for improved student achievement is the classroom, it's insufficient for teachers to have access to curricula derived from the state standards. Teachers must also have access to a succinct and accurate interpretation of each of the standards to be taught and assessed. Why? Many of the standards are so complex that they are subject to divergent interpretations, much like state and federal laws. Teachers, teacher leaders, school leaders, curriculum writers, and central office personnel who support schools must also have access to a succinct and accurate interpretation of the standards to be taught and assessed Why? Teachers need the interpretation of the standards to ensure that their planning and subsequent instruction is consistently aligned to the nuanced expectations of the standards. Teacher leaders, school leaders, curriculum writers, and central office personnel who support schools must have access to the interpretation of the standards so that they are able to provide meaningful feedback to teachers and make appropriate decisions for curricular programming.

Since we are in a dialogue about unpacking standards allow me to use a bit of sarcasm to pose another rhetorical question. Teachers, teacher leaders, school leaders, curriculum writers, and central office personnel have been unpacking the state standards for years. At what point will they be unpacked once and for all?—Because that would be a day worth celebrating. This chapter is designed to get schools/districts closer to that great day of celebration. The remaining pages of this chapter are excerpts from the catalogue of 33 teacher resource books that I have published to assist educators in their effort to fully understand the standards and consequently sharpen their individual and collective ability to provide students with instruction that promotes mastery of the content and ultimately position children for choice-filled lives.

For illustrative purposes, I included interpretations of a limited number of English/Language Arts standards. I selected one informational text standard [RI2] and interpreted it from kindergarten to grade 12 so that you can see how the expectations shift from one grade to the next and from one grade band to the next.

In the appendix, I have included a second and third set of materials. The second set being an excerpt of standards-aligned, next generation English/Language Arts graphic organizers for RI2 and the third being a set of standards-aligned mathematics graphic organizers, excerpted from Educational Epiphany's comprehensive catalogue of teacher and student resources. The excerpted graphic organizers are for a single domain for grades 3, 5, and 7 so that you can see the focus, coherence, procedural fluency, conceptual understanding, application, and dual intensity elements built in to the instructional materials.

You will readily notice that the content in this chapter and in the appendix was written to support teacher capacity to provide instruction aligned to the standards. I did not recycle content, I had to begin with a blank page and a single standard and build from nothing to something worth consuming.

Each English/Language Arts interpretation guide page includes:

- a grade-level standard that we know will be assessed,

- the nuanced interpretation of a standard and common misconceptions,

- standards-aligned performance-based objective(s) to be taught and assessed,

- academic language of the standard and correlate operational definitions,

- standards-aligned essential questions that teachers should pose throughout the gradual release process to promote mastery, and

- important teacher reminders where appropriate.

Each English/Language Arts and Mathematics graphic organizer includes:

- a grade-level standard that we know will be assessed,

- a balanced procedural fluency and conceptual understanding map aligned to each element of the standard, to be used to teach and assess students developing understanding of a portion of a standard or a complete standard,

- academic language of the standard and correlate operational definitions, and

- notes and reminders where appropriate [See Appendix].

The content of this chapter and the appendix—Common Core, Non-Common Core, or Texas Essential Knowledge and Skills are an international model for standards interpretation. So much confusion exists relative to the true intentions of standards that student achievement is being caught in the crosshairs. The remainder of this chapter and the correlate content in the appendix will advance and bring clarity to this important international dialogue.

Kindergarten

State Standard:

RI K.2—With prompting and support, identify the main topic (subject) and retell key details of a text (important details).

Interpretation of Standard:

Part 1: Students must learn to distinguish between ancillary and important words or phrases in order to (1) restate them and (2) explain how the key details support the main topic of an informational text.

Part 2: Answers the question, "What is subject of the text?" Not to be conflated with main idea, which answers the question, "What is the text mostly about?" Main idea enters the standards in grade 3.

Performance-Based Objective:

- SWBAT identify and retell key details IOT determine the main topic of a text.

Academic Language:

Author	the person who wrote the text
Determine	to conclude or ascertain after reasoning
Identify	recognize and name
Key Details	important words or phrases
Main Topic	the central subject of the text
Phrase	a sequence of words intended to have meaning
Prompt	to assist by suggesting; cue
Retell	recount; tell again
Support	to hold up; reinforce

GUIDING QUESTIONS

1. What is the main topic of this text?
2. Which key details in this text helped you to learn more about the main topic?

Grade 1

State Standard:

RI 1.2—Identify the main topic (subject) and retell key details of a text (important details).

Interpretation of Standard:

Part 1: Students must learn to distinguish between ancillary and important words or phrases in order to (1) restate them and (2) explain how the key details support the main topic of an informational text.

Part 2: Answers the question, "What is subject of the text?" Not to be conflated with main idea, which answers the question, "What is the text mostly about?" Main idea enters the standards in grade 3.

Performance-Based Objective:

- SWBAT identify and retell key details IOT determine the main topic of a text.

Academic Language:

Author	the person who wrote the text
Determine	to conclude or ascertain after reasoning
Identify	recognize and name
Key Details	important words or phrases
Main Topic	the central subject of the text
Phrase	a sequence of words intended to have meaning
Prompt	to assist by suggesting; cue
Retell	recount; tell again
Support	to hold up; reinforce

GUIDING QUESTIONS

1. What is the main topic of this text?
2. Which key details in this text helped you to learn more about the main topic?
3. Retell the key details from the beginning to the end of this text.

Grade 2

State Standard:

RI 2.2—Identify the main topic of a multi-paragraph text as well as the focus of specific paragraphs within the text.

Interpretation of Standard:

Identifying the topic answers the question, "What is subject of the text?" Not to be conflated with main idea, which answers the question, "What is the text mostly about?" Main idea is a grade three skill.

Student must be required to determine the focus of different paragraphs within the multi-paragraph text. Students should be able to make connections between the focus of each paragraph and the topic of the entire text.

Performance-Based Objective:

• SWBAT identify key details IOT determine the main topic of a multi-paragraph text.

• SWBAT identify the main topic of a multi-paragraph text IOT determine the focus of specific paragraphs within a text.

Academic Language:

Determine	to conclude or ascertain after reasoning
Focus	thing or place that is of greatest interest or importance
Identify	recognize and name
Key Details	important words or phrases
Main Topic	the central subject of the text
Multi-paragraph	more than one paragraph
Retell	recount; tell again
Support	to hold up; reinforce

GUIDING QUESTIONS

1. What is the main topic of the text?
2. What are the key details in the text that support the main topic?
3. What is a focus?
4. What is the focus of each paragraph?
5. How does each paragraph connect to the main topic?

Grade 3

State Standard:

RI 3.2—Determine the main idea of a text; recount the key details and explain how they support the main idea.

Interpretation of Standard:

Students should be able to determine what the text is mostly about. Students should be able to distinguish between the main idea and the topic/subject of the text, which is too broad to be the main idea. Too broad as a concept must be taught and it must be associated with the topic of the text.

Students should be aware that: (1) the main idea of text is not always found in the first sentence of a text, in fact, it is seldom found there; (2) in some cases the main idea is not stated at all; and (3) key details are too narrow to be the main idea. Too narrow as a concept must be taught and it must be associated with key details in the text.

In order to support their determination of the main idea, students will need a great deal of practice with distinguishing between ancillary and important words or phrases in order to explain how the key details support the development of the main idea.

Performance-Based Objective:

*   **SWBAT** identify and recount key details IOT determine the main idea of a text.

*   **SWBAT** identify the main idea of a text IOT explain how it is supported by key details.

Academic Language:

Determine	to conclude or ascertain after reasoning
Explain	to make something clear by describing it in more details or by revealing relevant facts or ideas
Identify	recognize and name
Key Details	important words or phrases
Main Topic	the central subject of the text
Multi-paragraph	more than one paragraph
Topic	the central subject of the text
Recount	retell; tell again
Support	to hold up; reinforce

GUIDING QUESTIONS

1. Define main idea.
2. Define topic.
3. How is topic different than main idea?
4. Define key detail.
5. Which is too broad to be the main idea, a topic or a key detail?
6. Which is too narrow to be the main idea, a topic or a key detail?
7. What is the topic of this text?
8. Define support.
9. What do key details have to do with determining the main idea of an informational text?
10. Define support.
11. What is the main idea of this text?
12. Which key details supported the development of the main idea of this text?

Grade 4

Interpretation of Standard:

RI 4.2—Determine the main idea of a text and explain how it is supported by key details; summarize the text.

Interpretation of Standard:

Students should be able to determine what the text is mostly about. Students should be able to distinguish between the main idea and the topic/subject of the text, which is too broad to be the main idea. Too broad as a concept must be taught and it must be associated with the topic of the text.

Students should be aware that: (1) the main idea of text is not always found in the first sentence of a text, in fact, it is seldom found there; (2) in some cases the main idea is not stated at all; and (3) key details are too narrow to be the main idea. Too narrow as a concept must be taught and it must be associated with key details in the text.

In order to support their determination of the main idea, students will need a great deal of practice with distinguishing between ancillary and important words or phrases in order to explain how the key details support the development of the main idea.

In order to master this skill, students must understand that a summary is a brief statement that contains the essential ideas of a longer passage, not to be conflated with a paraphrase, which is a restatement of the source text in about the same number of words.

Performance-Based Objective:

- SWBAT identify key details IOT determine the main idea of a text.

- SWBAT identify the main idea of a text IOT explain how it is supported by key details.

- SWBAT identify the main idea of a text IOT compose a summary.

Academic Language:

Compose	write or create
Determine	to conclude or ascertain after reasoning
Explain	to make something clear by describing it in more details or by revealing relevant facts or ideas

Identify	recognize and name
Key Details	important words or phrases
Main Topic	the central subject of the text
Paraphrase	a restatement of the source text in about the same number of words
Recount	retell; tell again
Summary	a brief statement that contains the essential ideas of a longer passage
Support	to hold up; reinforce
Topic	the central subject of the text

GUIDING QUESTIONS

1. Define main idea.
2. Define topic.
3. How is topic different than main idea?
4. Define key detail.
5. Which is too broad to be the main idea, a topic or a key detail?
6. Which is too narrow to be the main idea, a topic or a key detail?
7. What is the topic of this text?
8. Define support.
9. What do key details have to do with determining the main idea of an informational text?
10. What is the main idea of this text?
11. Which key details supported the development of the main idea of this text?
12. Define summary.
13. What are the components of a summary?
14. Define paraphrase?
15. What is the difference between paraphrasing and summarizing?
16. Compose a summary this text.

Grade 5

State Standard:

RI 5.2—Determine two or more main ideas of a text and explain how they are supported by key details; summarize the text.

Interpretation of Standard:

Students should be able to determine what the text is mostly about. Students should be able to distinguish between the main idea and the topic/subject of the text, which is too broad to be the main idea. Too broad as a concept must be taught and it must be associated with the topic of the text.

Students should be aware that: (1) the main idea of text is not always found in the first sentence of a text, in fact, it is seldom found there; (2) in some cases the main idea is not stated at all; and (3) key details are too narrow to be the main idea. Too narrow as a concept must be taught and it must be associated with key details in the text.

In order to support their determination of the main idea, students will need a great deal of practice with distinguishing between ancillary and important words or phrases in order to explain how the key details support the development of the main idea.

In order to master this skill, students must understand that a summary is a brief statement that contains the essential ideas of a longer passage, not to be conflated with a paraphrase, which is a restatement of the source text in about the same number of words.

Performance-Based Objective:

- SWBAT identify key details IOT determine 2 or more main ideas of a text.

- SWBAT identify two or more main ideas of a text IOT explain how they are supported by key details.

- SWBAT identify the main ideas of a text IOT compose a summary.

Academic Language:

Compose	write or create
Determine	to conclude or ascertain after reasoning
Explain	to make something clear by describing it in more details or by revealing relevant facts or ideas

Identify	recognize and name
Key Details	important words or phrases
Main Idea	what the text is mostly about
Paraphrase	a restatement of the source text in about the same number of words
Recount	retell; tell again
Summary	a brief statement that contains the essential ideas of a longer passage
Support	to hold up; reinforce
Topic	the central subject of the text

GUIDING QUESTIONS

1. Define main idea.
2. Define topic.
3. How is topic different than main idea?
4. Define key detail.
5. Which is too broad to be the main idea, a topic or a key detail?
6. Which is too narrow to be the main idea, a topic or a key detail?
7. What is the topic of this text?
8. Define support.
9. What do key details have to do with determining the main idea(s) of an informational text?
10. What are the main ideas of this text?
11. Which key details supported the development of the main ideas of this text?
12. Define summary.
13. What are the components of a summary?
14. Define paraphrase?
15. What is the difference between paraphrasing and summarizing?
16. Compose a summary this text with attention to the essential ideas presented in the text.

Grade 6

State Standard:

RI 6.2—Determine a central idea of a text and how it is conveyed through particular details; provide a summary of the text distinct from personal opinions or judgments.

Interpretation of Standard:

Students should be able to determine the thought, concept, notion, or impression that is of greatest importance of portions (chapters, pages, sections, paragraphs are mostly about) a given text. Students should be able to distinguish between the central idea of specific portions of a text and the topic/subject of the text, which is too broad to be a central idea. Too broad as a concept must be taught and it must be associated with the topic of the text.

Central idea is synonymous with the concept of main idea (what the text or portion of a text is mostly about). This is the main idea standard that was taught in grades 3-5. Central idea replaces main idea in grade 6. Central idea is NOT synonymous with literary central idea, which is akin to theme. This is informational text central idea, which is: the thought, concept, notion, or impression that is of greatest importance.

Students should be aware that: (1) the central ideas of text are not always found in the first sentence of a given paragraph, in fact, the central idea is seldom found there; (2) in some cases the central ideas are not stated at all; and (3) key details are too narrow to be a central idea. Too narrow as a concept must be taught and it must be associated with key details in the text.

In order to support their determination of central ideas, students will need a great deal of practice with distinguishing between ancillary and important words or phrases in order to explain how the key details support the development of a central idea.

In order to master this skill, students must understand that a summary is a brief statement that contains the essential ideas of a longer passage, not to be conflated with a paraphrase, which is a restatement of the source text in about the same number of words.

Students are required to summarize texts without including their personal opinions and judgments on the topic; doing so may difficult for students because, for years, they have been asked to make text-to-self connections.

Performance-Based Objective:

- **SWBAT** identify key details IOT determine the central idea of a text.

- **SWBAT** determine the central idea IOT explain how it is conveyed through particular details.

- **SWBAT** determine the central idea IOT compose a summary distinct from personal opinions and judgments.

Academic Language:

Central Idea	the thought, concept, notion, or impression that is of greatest importance in the text or potion of the text, it may be implied or explicitly stated
Compose	write or create
Convey	to communicate or make known
Determine	to conclude or ascertain after reasoning
Development	growing and becoming more mature, advanced, or elaborate
Distinct	separate or different from
Explain	to make something clear by describing it in more details or by revealing relevant facts or ideas
Identify	recognize and name
Judgment	an informed and objective opinion formulated without bias
Key Details	important words or phrases
Main Idea	what the text is mostly about
Paraphrase	a restatement of the source text in about the same number of words
Particular	specific
Personal Opinion	a belief or conclusion held with confidence, but not substantiated by proof
Phrase	small group of related words within a sentence or a clause; a group of two or more words that expresses a single idea but does not form a complete sentence

Summary	a brief statement that contains the essential ideas of a longer passage
Support	to hold up; reinforce
Topic	the central subject of the text

GUIDING QUESTIONS

1. Define central idea.
2. Define topic.
3. How is topic different than central idea?
4. Define key detail.
5. Which is too broad to be a central idea, a topic or a key detail?
6. Which is too narrow to be a central idea, a topic or a key detail?
7. What is the topic of this text?
8. Define support.
9. What do key details have to do with conveying the central ideas of an informational text?
10. What are the central ideas of this text?
11. Which key details conveyed the central ideas of this text?
12. Define summary.
13. What are the components of a summary?
14. Define paraphrase?
15. What is the difference between paraphrasing and summarizing?
16. Define distinct.
17. Define personal opinion.
18. Define judgment.
19. Compose a summary this text with attention to the essential ideas presented in the text. Be sure to compose the summary distinct of personal opinions and judgments.

Grade 7

State Standard:

RI 7.2—Determine two or more central ideas in a text and analyze their development over the course of the text; provide an objective summary of the text.

Interpretation of Standard:

Students should be able to determine what specific portions (chapters, pages, sections, paragraphs are mostly about. Students should be able to distinguish between the central idea (the thought, concept, notion, or impression that is of greatest importance in the text or potion of the text) of specific portions of a text and the topic (subject) of the text, which is too broad to be a central idea. Too broad as a concept must be taught and it must be associated with the topic of the text.

Students should be aware that: (1) the central ideas of text are not always found in the first sentence of a given paragraph, in fact, the central idea is seldom found there; (2) in some cases the central ideas are not stated at all; and (3) key details are too narrow to be a central idea. Too narrow as a concept must be taught and it must be associated with key details in the text.

Central idea as used in this informational text standard is synonymous with the concept of main idea (what the text or portion of a text is mostly about) that was taught in the informational text standards in grades 3-5. Central idea replaces main idea in grade 6. Central idea is NOT synonymous with literary central idea, which is akin to theme. This is informational text central idea, which is: the thought, concept, notion, or impression that is of greatest importance.

In order to support their determination of central ideas, students will need a great deal of practice with distinguishing between ancillary and important words or phrases in order to explain how the key details support the development of a central idea.

Students must also understand that a summary is a brief statement that contains the essential ideas of a longer passage, not to be conflated with a paraphrase, which is a restatement of the source text in about the same number of words.

Students are required to summarize texts without including their personal opinions and judgments on the topic; doing so may difficult for students because, for years, they have been asked to make text-to-self connections.

Performance-Based Objective:

- SWBAT identify key details IOT determine 2 or more central ideas of a text.

- SWBAT identify 2 or more central ideas of a text IOT analyze their development over the course of a text.

- SWBAT identify the central ideas of a text IOT compose a summary

Academic Language:

Central Idea	the thought, concept, notion, or impression that is of greatest importance in the text or potion of the text, it may be implied or explicitly stated
Citation	a reference from a text brought forward as a support (more useful when it includes the line number, page number, paragraph number, and/or author—especially when reading more than one text on the same topic or theme)
Compose	to write or create
Determine	to conclude or ascertain after reasoning
Development	growing and becoming more mature, advanced, or elaborate
Distinct	separate or different from
Explain	to make something clear by describing it in more details or by revealing relevant facts or ideas
Identify	recognize and name
Judgment	an informed and objective opinion formulated without bias
Key Details	important words or phrases
Paraphrase	a restatement of the source text in about the same number of words
Personal Opinion	a belief or conclusion held with confidence, but not substantiated by proof

Summary	a brief statement that contains the essential ideas of a longer passage
Topic	the central subject of the text

GUIDING QUESTIONS

1. Define identify.
2. What are key details?
3. Define determine.
4. Define central idea.
5. Define topic.
6. How is topic different than central idea?
7. What is the topic of this text?
8. Which one is too narrow to be a central idea: the topic or a key detail?
9. Which one is too broad to be a central idea: the topic or a key detail?
10. What are the central ideas of this informational text? Be sure to identify key details to support your response.
11. Define analyze.
12. Define development.
13. Select one of the central ideas of the text. What key details did the author use to develop that central idea over the course of the text?
14. Define compose.
15. Define summary.
16. Compose a summary of the text. Be sure to use the essential ideas of the passage to develop your summary. Do not include personal opinions or judgments in the summary.

Grade 8

State Standard:

RI 8.2—Determine a central idea of a text and analyze its development over the course of the text, including its relationship to supporting ideas; provide an objective summary of the text.

Interpretation of Standard:

Students should be able to determine what specific portions (chapters, pages, sections, paragraphs are mostly about. Students should be able to distinguish between the central idea (the thought, concept, notion, or impression that is of greatest importance in the text or potion of the text) of specific portions of a text and the topic (subject) of the text, which is too broad to be the central idea. Too broad as a concept must be taught and it must be associated with the topic of the text.

Students should be aware that: (1) the central idea of a text is not always found in the first sentence of a given paragraph, in fact, the central idea is seldom found there; (2) in some cases the central idea is not stated at all; and (3) key details are too narrow to be the central idea. Too narrow as a concept must be taught and it must be associated with key details in the text.

Central idea as used in this informational text standard is synonymous with the concept of main idea (what the text or portion of a text is mostly about) that was taught in the informational text standards in grades 3-5. Central idea replaces main idea in grade 6. Central idea is NOT synonymous with literary central idea, which is akin to theme. This is informational text central idea, which is: the thought, concept, notion, or impression that is of greatest importance.

In order to support their determination of central idea, students will need a great deal of practice with distinguishing between ancillary and important words or phrases in order to explain how the key details support the development of a central idea over the course of the text.

Students must also understand that a summary is a brief statement that contains the essential ideas of a longer passage, not to be conflated with a paraphrase, which is a restatement of the source text in about the same number of words.

Students are required to write an objective summary (without including their personal opinions and judgments on the topic); doing so may difficult for students because, for years, they have been asked to make text-to-self connections.

Performance-Based Objective:

- SWBAT identify key details IOT determine the central idea of a text.

- SWBAT identify the central idea IOT analyze its relationship to supporting ideas.

- SWBAT identify the central idea of a text IOT analyze its development over the course of a text.

Academic Language:

Central Idea	the thought, concept, notion, or impression that is of greatest importance in the text or potion of the text, it may be implied or explicitly stated
Citation	a reference from a text brought forward as a support (more useful when it includes the line number, page number, paragraph number, and/or author—especially when reading more than one text on the same topic or theme)
Compose	to write or create
Determine	to conclude or ascertain after reasoning
Development	growing and becoming more mature, advanced, or elaborate
Distinct	separate or different from
Explain	to make something clear by describing it in more details or by revealing relevant facts or ideas
Identify	recognize and name
Judgment	an informed and objective opinion formulated without bias
Key Details	important words or phrases
Paraphrase	a restatement of the source text in about the same number of words
Personal Opinion	a belief or conclusion held with confidence, but not substantiated by proof
Relationship	connection
Supporting ideas	thoughts, concepts, or notions that hold up or serve as the foundation of a larger/more broad idea

Summary	a brief statement that contains the essential ideas of a longer passage
Topic	the central subject of the text

GUIDING QUESTIONS

1. Define identify.
2. What are key details?
3. Define determine.
4. Define central idea.
5. Define topic.
6. How is topic different than central idea?
7. What is the topic of this text?
8. Which one is too narrow to be a central idea: the topic or a key detail?
9. Which one is too broad to be a central idea: the topic or a key detail?
10. What is the central idea of this informational text? Be sure to identify key details to support your response.
11. Define analyze.
12. Define relationship.
13. Define supporting ideas.
14. What is the relationship between the relationship between the central idea and supporting ideas?
15. Define development.
16. What is the central idea of the text? What key details did the author use to develop that central idea over the course of the text?
17. Define compose.
18. Define summary.
19. Compose a summary of the text. Be sure to use the essential ideas of the passage to develop your summary. Do not include personal opinions or judgments in the summary. The summary must be objective.

Grade 9

State Standard:

RI 9.2/10.2—Determine a central idea of a text and analyze its development over the course of the text, including how it emerges and is shaped and refined by specific details; provide an objective summary of the text.

Interpretation of Standard:

Students should be able to determine what specific portions (chapters, pages, sections, paragraphs are mostly about. Students should be able to distinguish between the central idea (the thought, concept, notion, or impression that is of greatest importance in the text or potion of the text) of specific portions of a text and the topic (subject) of the text, which is too broad to be the central idea. Too broad as a concept must be taught and it must be associated with the topic of the text.

Students should be aware that: (1) the central idea of a text is not always found in the first sentence of a given paragraph, in fact, the central idea is seldom found there; (2) in some cases the central idea is not stated at all; and (3) key details are too narrow to be the central idea. Too narrow as a concept must be taught and it must be associated with key details in the text.

Central idea as used in this informational text standard is synonymous with the concept of main idea (what the text or portion of a text is mostly about) that was taught in the informational text standards in grades 3-5. Central idea replaces main idea in grade 6. Central idea is NOT synonymous with literary central idea, which is akin to theme. This is informational text central idea, which is: the thought, concept, notion, or impression that is of greatest importance.

In order to support their determination of central idea, students will need a great deal of practice with distinguishing between ancillary and important words or phrases in order to explain how the key details support the development of a central idea over the course of the text. Once the central idea has been determined, students will need to go back to the text to identify specific details that help the central idea to emerge (get introduced), shape (evolve), and get refined (become clearer/fully developed).

Students must also understand that a summary is a brief statement that contains the essential ideas of a longer passage, not to be conflated with a paraphrase, which is a restatement of the source text in about the same number of words.

Students are required to write an objective summary (without including their personal opinions and judgments on the topic); doing so may difficult for students because, for years, they have been asked to make text-to-self connections.

Performance-Based Objective:

- SWBAT identify key details IOT determine the central idea of a text.

- SWBAT determine the central idea of a text IOT analyze its development over the course of the text, including how it emerges, is shaped, and is refined by specific details.

- SWBAT identify the central idea of a text IOT compose an objective summary.

Academic Language:

Analyze	to break into smaller components for the purpose of study or examination
Central Idea	the thought, concept, notion, or impression that is of greatest importance in the text or potion of the text, it may be implied or explicitly stated
Citation	a reference from a text brought forward as a support (more useful when it includes the line number, page number, paragraph number, and/or author—especially when reading more than one text on the same topic or theme)
Compose	to write or create
Determine	to conclude or ascertain after reasoning
Development	growing and becoming more mature, advanced, or elaborate
Distinct	separate or different from
Essential	absolutely necessary; extremely important
Explain	to make something clear by describing it in more details or by revealing relevant facts or ideas
Identify	recognize and name

Judgment	an informed and objective opinion formulated without bias
Key Details	important words or phrases
Paraphrase	a restatement of the source text in about the same number of words
Personal Opinion	a belief or conclusion held with confidence, but not substantiated by proof
Refine	to improve by making small changes
Shape	the act of providing more information on an idea, including establishing relevance/context
Summary	a brief statement that contains the essential ideas of a longer passage
Topic	the central subject of the text

GUIDING QUESTIONS

1. Define identify.
2. What are key details?
3. Define determine.
4. Define central idea.
5. Define topic.
6. How is topic different than central idea?
7. What is the topic of this text?
8. Which one is too narrow to be a central idea: the topic or a key detail?
9. Which one is too broad to be a central idea: the topic or a key detail?
10. What is the central idea of this informational text? Be sure to identify key details to support your response.
11. Define analyze.
12. Define development.

GUIDING QUESTIONS (CONTINUED)

13. What is the central idea of this text again?
14. What key details does the author use to cause the central idea to emerge?
15. What key details does the author use to shape the central idea?
16. What key details does the author use to refine the central idea?
17. Define compose.
18. Define summary.
19. Compose a summary of the text. Be sure to use the essential ideas of the passage to develop your summary. Do not include personal opinions or judgments in the summary. The summary must be objective.

Grades 11–12

State Standard:

RI 11.2/12.2—Determine two or more central ideas of a text and analyze their development over the course of the text, including how they interact and build on one another to provide a complex analysis; provide an objective summary of the text.

Interpretation of Standard:

Students should be able to determine to or more concepts, thoughts, notions, or impressions of greatest importance in the text (of chapters, pages, sections, paragraphs). Students should be able to distinguish between central idea (the thought, concept, notion, or impression that is of greatest importance in the text or potion of the text) of specific portions of a text and the topic (subject) of the text, which is too broad to be the central idea. Too broad as a concept must be taught and it must be associated with the topic of the text.

Students should be aware that: (1) central ideas are not always found in the first sentence of a given paragraph, in fact, central ideas are seldom found there; (2) in some cases central ideas is not stated at all; and (3) key details are too narrow to be a central idea. Too narrow as a concept must be taught and it must be associated with key details in the text.

Central idea as used in this informational text standard is synonymous with the concept of main idea (what the text or portion of a text is mostly about) that was taught in the informational text standards in grades 3-5. Central idea replaces main idea in grade 6. Central idea is NOT synonymous with literary central idea, which is akin to theme. This is informational text central idea, which is: the thought, concept, notion, or impression that is of greatest importance.

In order to support their determination of central idea, students will need a great deal of practice with distinguishing between ancillary and important words or phrases in order to explain how the key details support the development of a central idea over the course of the text. Once a central idea has been determined, students will need to go back to the text to analyze the development of the central ideas over the course of the text, including how they interact with one another and build upon one another to create a complex text/set of ideas.

Students must also understand that a summary is a brief statement that contains the essential ideas of a longer passage, not to be conflated with a paraphrase, which is a restatement of the source text in about the same number of words.

Students are required to write an objective summary (without including their personal opinions and judgments on the topic); doing so may difficult for students because, for years, they have been asked to make text-to-self connections.

Performance-Based Objective:

- **SWBAT** identify key details IOT determine 2 or more central ideas of a text.

- **SWBAT** identify 2 or more central ideas of a text IOT analyze their development over the course of the text, including how they interact and build upon one another to provide a complex analysis.

- **SWBAT** identify 2 or more central ideas of a text IOT compose an objective summary.

Academic Language:

Analysis	the act of breaking into smaller components for the purpose of study or examination
Analyze	to break into smaller components for the purpose of study or examination
Central Idea	the thought, concept, notion, or impression that is of greatest importance in the text or potion of the text, it may be implied or explicitly stated
Citation	a reference from a text brought forward as a support (more useful when it includes the line number, page number, paragraph number, and/or author—especially when reading more than one text on the same topic or theme)
Complex	a group of things that are connected in complicated ways
Compose	to write or create

Determine	to conclude or ascertain after reasoning
Development	growing and becoming more mature, advanced, or elaborate
Distinct	separate or different from
Essential	absolutely necessary; extremely important
Explain	to make something clear by describing it in more details or by revealing relevant facts or ideas
Identify	recognize and name
Interact	to come together and have an effect on each other
Judgment	an informed and objective opinion formulated without bias
Key Details	important words or phrases
Objective	not influenced by personal feelings or opinions in considering or representing facts
Paraphrase	a restatement of the source text in about the same number of words
Personal Opinion	a belief or conclusion held with confidence, but not substantiated by proof
Summary	a brief statement that contains the essential ideas of a longer passage
Topic	the central subject of the text

GUIDING QUESTIONS

1. Define identify.
2. What are key details?
3. Define determine.
4. Define central idea.
5. Define topic.
6. How is topic different than central idea?
7. What is the topic of this text?
8. Which one is too narrow to be a central idea: the topic or a key detail?
9. Which one is too broad to be a central idea: the topic or a key detail?
10. What is one of the central ideas of this informational text? Be sure to identify key details to support your response.
11. What is another central idea of this informational text? Be sure to identify key details to support your response.
12. If there is a third central idea of this informational text, what is it? Be sure to identify key details to support your response.
13. How do the central ideas build on one another over the course of the informational text?
14. How do the central ideas interact with one another over the course of the informational text to provide a complex set of ideas?
15. Define compose.
16. Define summary.
17. Compose a summary of the text. Be sure to use the essential ideas of the passage to develop your summary. Do not include personal opinions or judgments in the summary. The summary must be objective.

CHAPTER SIX

Ensure Rigorous Instructon Through Explicit Instruction Characterized by Cognitive Pluralism

> " *It's not the neighborhood that fosters underachievement, rather it's the instruction in the neighborhood that nurtures underachievement.* "

When did rigor become a four-letter word? What ever happened to rigor? Where did it go? I know what happened. Much like the 'high expectations," I believe that teachers, teacher leaders, school leaders, curriculum writers, and central office personnel who support schools have so many definitions of rigor that we have been unable to calibrate around it for far too long. Permit me to offer a simple operational definition for rigor. Cognitive Pluralism + Gradual Release = Rigor. One caveat. I do not believe that science instruction should be characterized by gradual release, but I will address that assertion later in this chapter. For science, Cognitive Pluralism + The 5Es = Rigor.

In classrooms across the nation, teachers require students to memorize content-related facts, as they should. In science, students learn that matter exists in three phases. In English, students learn to identify commonly used literary devices. In social studies, students memorize the antecedents of the Boston Tea Party. But, all too often, to the detriment of student achievement, a vital component of instruction is lacking from daily instruction. That vital component is cognitive pluralism.

I remember instruction from my primary and secondary schooling days in a small town just outside Houston, Texas [Texas City, Texas]. Although I was enrolled in a gifted-education social studies course, my social studies teacher simply required us to memorize the constituent elements of the U.S. Constitution. More than three decades later, I can regurgitate facts about the structure of the seminal, historical document. The U.S. Constitution consists of a preamble, seven articles, signers, and amendments. But so what? What did I gain beyond an ability to retain the aforementioned facts?

My social studies teacher not only neglected to teach my classmates and I to approach historical texts as if we were historians – attending to credibility and bias as well as the interaction between and among individuals, events, and ideas, she also neglected to expose us to curriculum-driven opportunities to use our knowledge of the constituent elements of the U.S. Constitution to ascend the pyramid of cognitive demand. She should have required us to do something with our knowledge of the components of the constitution. That would have been rigorous instruction. Instead, we were relegated to instruction that taught us to regurgitate information (content) in the same manner in which it was disseminated, largely from a single source—that anthology of a textbook. We were not required to use our new knowledge to perform a meaningful and relevant task. She was a very nice teacher and we loved her class, but in retrospect, the instruction we received was one-dimensional. This classroom archetype still exists in districts all over the nation.

Over four decades ago, Benjamin Bloom headed a group of educational psychologists who developed a classification of levels of intellectual behavior salient to the process of teaching and learning. Bloom (1956) found that over 95% of the questions students were asked only required them to think at the lowest possible level...information recall [Sounds an awful lot like my primary and secondary experience]. Bloom identified six levels of cognition within the cognitive domain, from the simplest—recall or recognition of facts through increasingly more complex and abstract mental levels, to the highest level—which is now classified as creating. Although Blooms' research has been widely accepted as useful for the purpose of planning and facilitating instruction representative of cognitive pluralism, many schools/districts have yet to find ways to integrate what they know about cognitive pluralism into curricula, instructional materials, instructional practice, and assessment opportunities. This brief, but critical chapter, will delineate the actionable steps for composing performance-based objectives that will invariably promote higher levels of thinking and doing for all students regardless of ability.

The following simple changes in the delivery of instruction on the U.S. Constitution would have taken my teacher's instruction from mediocre to rigorous, authentic, intellectual work. She should have required us to:

1. use our knowledge of the structure of the U.S. Constitution to compare and contrast it to the Magna Carta,

2. compare and contrast the function of the U.S. Constitution and the Magna Carta,

3. trace and explain the influence of the Magna Carta on modern constitutional law in the English speaking and non-English speaking world,

4. evaluate the effectiveness of the U.S. Constitution's structure and clarity of word choice, and

5. create a new and improved constitution for a newly formed society using the U.S. Constitution and Magna Carta as guides.

Requiring students to engage in the aforementioned activities requires students to recall information; demonstrate a conceptual understanding of the content; apply newly acquired knowledge to solve a real-world problem; analyze the parts of a whole; evaluate ideas and make judgments; and construct a new product [in this case, a fictitious document]. All students, regardless of race/ethnicity, socio-economic status, English proficiency and exceptionality should be exposed to such instruction on a daily basis—instruction of the highest quality. To that end, I recommend that instructional objectives are "performance-based" and consist of a "know" and a "do."

Table 6:1—Characteristics of Performance-Based Objectives for English/Language Arts, Social Studies, Science, and the Technical Subjects

	Performance-Based Objective Characteristic	Description
1	A "know"	The "know" represents the prerequisite content-related knowledge or skill that students must have or know in order to be able to demonstrate mastery of the "do" portion of the objective.
2	A "do"	A "do" The "do" represents that which students are expected to be able to do independently by the close of a lesson or a series of lessons. The "do" portion of an English/Language Arts, Social Studies, Science and the Technical Subjects performance-based objective should always be linked to a literacy skill that we know will be assessed and/or a higher- order thinking skill.

Table 6:2—Characteristics of Performance-Based Objectives for Mathematics

	Performance-Based Objective Characteristic	Description
1	A "know"	A "know" The "know" represents the prerequisite content-related knowledge or skill that students must have or know in order to be able to demonstrate mastery of the "do" portion of the objective.
2	A "do"	A "do" The "do" represents that which students are expected to be able to do independently by the close of a lesson or a series of lessons. The "do" portion of a Mathematics performance-based objective should always be linked to a worthwhile mathematical task [which is a higher-order thinking skill].

Below are some objectives that I have collected from the field that do not meet the gold standard for performance-based objectives. Following each objective is a critique against the Integrated Approach criteria, a possible rewrite, and an explanation of the rewrite—all of which is model feedback for teachers and school leaders.

Objective 1:

Students will be able to use a jigsaw to state the main idea of a portion of a text.

Critique:

Yes, students do need to know how to state the main idea of a portion of a text, that is a useful skill, but what does that skill have to do with using a jigsaw? It is plausible for a teacher to use an activity like a jigsaw as a vehicle to teach skills and assess student understanding of content/concepts. However, the word 'jigsaw' has no place in an objective. A jigsaw is an activity and it's likely that the jigsaw will become the focus of the lesson, diminishing the focus on the standards-based skill imbedded in this flawed objective—determining main idea of a portion of a text. Performance-based objectives must be comprised of a "know" related to the content/a standard, followed by an "in order to statement" which is the "do" that requires students to do something with their knowledge or skills.

Possible rewrite:

SWBAT identify the key details IOT determine the main idea of a portion of a text.

Explanation of rewrite:

- The "know" is identifying key details and the "do" is determining the main idea.

- The "know" is content-related prerequisite knowledge of the "do."

- The "do" is linked to a higher-order thinking skill—determining the main idea of a portion of a text.

Objective 2:
Students will be able to analyze the extent to which the author fulfills the writing purpose on page 62.

Critique:
The extent to which the author fulfills the writing purpose should be taught and assessed in English/Language Arts classes, but this objective does not include the prerequisite knowledge or skill that should accompany the higher-order task. Furthermore, the specific page number of the text to be used should not appear in the objective. Doing so may inadvertently impede student ability to view author's purpose as a skill that should be transferred beyond the reading opportunity on page 62 of that text. Examining the extent to which an author successfully fulfills the writing purpose is a universal skill that can be used to evaluate a text in any content area.

Rewrite:
SWBAT identify print features IOT analyze the extent to which the author fulfills the writing purpose.

Explanation of rewrite:
- The "know" is identifying print features and the "do" is analyzing the extent to which the author fulfills the writing purpose.

- The "know" is content-related prerequisite knowledge/skill for the "do."

- The "do" is linked to a higher-order thinking skill—analyzing the extent to which the author fulfills the writing purpose.

Objective 3:

SWBAT describe the Stamp Act as a cause of the American Revolution.

Critique:

The objective is "content-driven" much like the objectives from my own primary and secondary schooling and like the objectives in many classrooms across the nation. Undoubtedly, students should learn about the Stamp Act and they should know that it was related to the American Revolution, but this objective will only require students to memorize facts and does not represent cognitive pluralism.

Possible rewrite:

SWBAT describe the structure and function of the Stamp Act IOT formulate a bill for a legislative vote.

Explanation of rewrite:

- The "know" is describing the structure and function of the Stamp Act and the "do" is formulating a bill for a legislative vote. The word "function" in the rewrite promotes a discussion of the Stamp Act as a cause of the American Revolution.

- The "know" is content-related prerequisite knowledge of the "do."

- The "do" is linked to a higher-order thinking skill—formulating a bill for legislative consideration.

Below are example of objectives that meet the Performance-Based (Cognitively Plural) Criteria across grade levels and content areas:

1. SWBAT identify the parts of a cell IOT classify cells as plant or animal.

2. SWBAT identify the impact of Christianity on Ancient Rome IOT analyze the effects of religion on the larger society.

3. SWBAT identify the components of setting and plot IOT analyze details that contribute to meaning.

4. SWBAT graph pre-images and images under reflection and translation using a variety of tools (miras, pattypaper, Geometer's Sketchpad, and other virtual java tools) IOT interpret transformations as functions.

5. SWBAT identify the main idea of a text IOT compose an original paraphrase.

6. SWBAT cite relevant textual evidence IOT make inferences.

7. SWBAT analyze and draw conclusions about the magnitude of numbers using place value understanding IOT round whole numbers to the nearest 10 or 100.

8. SWBAT analyze word choice IOT determine the text structured used by an author to construct a given informational text.

9. SWBAT identify the main idea and key details IOT determine the author's purpose.

10. SWBAT identify the characteristic of all living things IOT classify and categorize organisms.

11. SWBAT find the greatest common factors of two whole numbers less than 100 IOT construct an equivalent numerical expression using the distributive property to express a sum of two whole numbers as a multiple of a sum of two whole numbers with no common factors.

12. SWBAT distinguish between potential and kinetic energy IOT explain the Law of Conservation of Energy.

13. SWBAT list and explain the main characteristics of a civilization IOT relate them to a hierarchy of human needs.

14. WBAT determine the meaning of words and phrases IOT interpret figurative language.

15. SWBAT evaluate square roots of perfect squares and the cube roots of perfect cubes IOT recognize and justify that $x2$ has 2 solutions (one positive and one negative) and that $x3$ has exactly 1 solution.

16. SWBAT analyze character traits IOT distinguish between dynamic and static characters.

17. SWBAT identify the process of genetic coding IOT compare inherited and acquired traits.

18. SWBAT use the properties of rational and irrational numbers IOT formulate a logical argument about the sum and product of different types of real numbers.

19. SWBAT rewrite expressions involving radicals using properties of addition, subtraction, and multiplication IOT generate equivalent expressions.

20. SWBAT analyze the leadership of selected European missionaries IOT compare them to leaders of modern society.

21. SWBAT rewrite expressions involving radicals using properties of addition, subtraction, and multiplication IOT generate equivalent expressions.

22. SWBAT find the rational approximation of irrational numbers IOT compare their size and approximate their location on the number line.

23. SWBAT analyze the Stamp Act IOT defend it as a major cause of the American Revolution.

24. SWBAT analyze the Magna Carta and the U.S. Constitution IOT compare and contrast documents central to the formulation of federal law.

25. SWBAT identify parts of an expression and analyze formulas and algebraic expressions from a given context IOT make sense of their multiple factors and terms by explaining the meaning of the individual parts in terms of the situations they models.

26. SWBAT identify bias in a given informational text IOT evaluate the reliability of information presented to the reader.

27. SWBAT read and write multi-digit whole numbers using base-ten numerals, number names, and expanded form IOT compare two multi-digit numbers based on meanings of the digits in each place, using $>$, $=$, and $<$.

28. SWBAT identify events of a given plot IOT analyze connections between characters, setting, and plot.

29. SWBAT to analyze primary sources IOT determine the influence, effect, or impact of historical, cultural, or biographical information on a text.

30. SWBAT write numbers and represent a number of objects with a written numeral from 0 to 20 IOT demonstrate their understanding of counting principles.

As it comes to the explicit instruction element of the formula for rigor, it is important to note that student achievement is a byproduct of thoughtful instructional planning. Masterfully written curricula, aligned perfectly to standards, do not guarantee student achievement and school improvement; rather I have found that it is the careful and deliberate delivery of instruction that results in bolstered student achievement. As, I stated in chapter two, a learning community with a true culture of instruction must rally around a common set of theories, standards, and practices. I would like to advance that discussion by suggesting vehemently that schools/districts consider the use a set of shift-aligned, content-sensitive lesson planning templates in order to facilitate the development of classroom instruction of the highest quality. Lesson plans that fail to align with the tenant of the culture of instruction will permit members of the team to talk a good game without being held accountable for playing a good game.

In the absence of an agreed upon, strategically-designed, lesson plan template for the core content areas, teacher leaders, school leaders, and central office personnel who support schools will have difficulty calibrating their feedback to teachers. Worse, without an agreed upon strategically-designed lesson plan template, teachers will be exponentially more likely to receive conflicting feedback and mixed messages from members of the site-based and district-level instructional leadership team.—You can guess who will be caught in the crosshairs of the conflicting feedback and mixed message. The children.

The Integrated Approach lesson plan templates are based on Gradual Release of Responsibility Model, the 5Es (for science only) and research-driven, instructional shifts discussed in chapter 4. Each template prompts teachers to plan and facilitate instruction that requires students gradually to take on more responsibility for knowledge development skills acquisition as the lesson progresses. The core of each lesson plan template concludes with a formative assessment in the independent setting and considerations for homework. Likewise, each lesson plan template prompts teachers to attend to content-specific imperatives.

For example:

- the **English/Language Arts** lesson plan template prompts teachers to pre-think their plan for engaging students to engage in a rich and rigorous evidence-based conversation and standards-based writing opportunity.

- the **social studies** lesson plan template prompts teachers to consider and pre-select the primary and secondary sources he/she might use to teach and assess students' understanding of an historical figure, era, or series of event;

- the **science** template does not promote the use of the gradual release model. Instead the science lesson plan template prompts teachers to take a non-linear approach to using the Five E's to plan the core of science instruction including: engagement, exploration, explanation, elaboration and evaluation; and

- the **mathematics** lesson plan template prompts teachers to consider identifying each practice problem to be used throughout the gradual release process and pre-working each of them to ensure that the problems are the best fit for teaching and assessing the concept(s) under study.

In the remaining pages of this chapter, you will find each of the suggested lesson plan templates chockfull with thoughtful content-specific reminders, prompts, and recommendations. Although they appear lengthy, they are not. Remove the reminders/prompts and only a couple of pages remain. I whole-heartedly endorse them. I have seen them transform lackluster, one-dimensional, standards-misaligned instruction to distinguished, rigorous, standards-aligned instruction—which is our reasonable service to other people's children.

Designing Performance-Based Instruction Aligned with the State Standards for English/Language Arts

Number of Days Needed to Teach to Mastery:

State Standard under Study:

Performance-Based Objective: (Objectives should be composed in the know and do format. The **"know"** refers to the content whereas the **"do"** refers to a literacy standard and/or a higher order thinking skill).

SWBAT

IOT

General and Domain Specific Vocabulary Words:

List and operationally define key terms that are essential to student mastery of the objective. (Students should be encouraged to use knowledge of Latin and Greek word parts and/or context clues to create meaning before and during reading).

What strategy(ies)/method(s) will be used to explicitly teach unfamiliar words and phrases in the performance-based objective and the text(s) to be used? Consider annotating each text.

Teacher Model: The teacher demonstrates what students should **know** and **be able to do** while students listen attentively, taking notes where appropriate.

Q1: What informational or literary text(s) will be used to model the skill? List the titles of each text to be used in the teacher model and note the portion of the text to be used if applicable.

Q2: Does the informational text support exposing students to a variety of historical, scientific, or technical texts across topics, eras, and/or perspectives? **OR**

Q3: Does the literary text support exposing students to a variety of authors, themes, genres (i.e., dramas, stories, poetry), and traditions (i.e., mythical, traditional, classical)?

Q4: What is the plan for exposing students to a rich and rigorous evidence-based conversation and writing opportunity during the model? **Suggestion:** Consider essential questions in resource and interpretation guide and graphic organizers.

Guided Practice: Students are asked to demonstrate developing knowledge of the objective by demonstrating their knowledge and ability in the large group setting. The teacher uses this opportunity to assess as many students as possible with special attention to struggling learners. This text/portion of the text can be written at the **instructional reading level** (grade level), since access to the text will be scaffold by the teacher. *If students are unsuccessful at this phase, then students would benefit from another teacher model.*

Q1: What informational or literary text(s) will be used to engage students in guided practice? List the titles of each text to be used throughout guided practice and note the portion of the text to be used if applicable.

Q2: Does the informational text expose students to a variety of historical, scientific, or technical texts across topics, eras, and/or perspectives? **OR**

Q3: Does the literary text expose students to a variety of authors, themes, genres (i.e., dramas, stories, poetry), and traditions (i.e., mythical, traditional, classical)?

Q4: What is the plan for engaging students in a rich and rigorous evidence-based conversation and writing opportunity during the guided practice? **Suggestion:** Consider essential questions in resource and interpretation guide and graphic organizers.

Collaborative Practice: Students are asked to work in groups of two to demonstrate developing knowledge of the objective. The teacher uses this opportunity to circulate the room assessing and assisting as many students as possible with special attention to struggling learners. This text/portion of the text should be written at the **independent level,** since students will be reading most of it without the teacher. *If students are successful in this phase, they are ready for the next step in the gradual release process.*

Q1: What informational or literary text(s) will be used to engage students in collaborative practice? List the titles of each text to be used for collaborative practice and note the portion of the text to be used if applicable.

Q2: Does the informational text expose students to a variety of historical, scientific, or technical texts across topics, eras, and/or perspectives? **OR**

Q3: Does the literary text expose students to a variety of authors, themes, genres (i.e., dramas, stories, poetry), and traditions (i.e., mythical, traditional, classical)?

Q4: What is the plan for requiring students to engage in a rich and rigorous evidence-based conversation and co-writing opportunity during the collaborative practice? **Suggestion:** Consider essential questions in resource and interpretation guide and graphic organizers.

Independent Practice: Students are asked to work independently to demonstrate knowledge of the objective. The teacher uses this opportunity to determine what students know and can do without any assistance from the teacher, teacher assistant, or peer. *If students are unsuccessful in this phase, then students may benefit from exposure to the general and domain specific vocabulary and/or exposure to a second round of the gradual release process.*

Q1: What informational or literary text(s) will be used to model the skill? List the titles of each text to be used for independent practice and note the portion of the text to be used if applicable.

Q2: Does the informational text expose students to a variety of historical, scientific, or technical texts across topics, eras, and/or perspectives? **OR**

Q3: Does the literary text expose students to a variety of authors, themes, genres (i.e., dramas, stories, poetry), and traditions (i.e., mythical, traditional, classical)?

Q4: What questions will students be required to answer? (Goal: To ensure that students can compose a rich evidence-based response?) **Suggestion:** Consider essential questions in resource and interpretation guide and graphic organizers.

Homework for Students Struggling with this Performance-Based Objective: (Students would benefit from homework aligned with the prerequisite skill necessary to demonstrate mastery of the know and do objective).

Homework for Students Not Struggling with this Performance-Based Objective: (Non- struggling students would benefit from homework designed to enrich their ability to apply knowledge and skills aligned with the know and do objective).

Designing Performance-Based Instruction Aligned with the State Standards for Social Studies

Number of Days Needed to Teach to Mastery:

State Standard Under Study:

Broad Social Studies Topic under Study/Broad Purpose for Learning:

Broad SS Topic or Broad Purpose	Check Category(ies) that Apply
Historical figure(s)	
Historical event(s)	
Conflict	
Cooperation	
Government	
Laws/rights	
Economics	
Period of time/era	
Region of the world	
Historical theme/phenomenon	
Resources (availability/impact)	

Performance-Based Objective: (Performance-Based Objectives should be composed in the **know and do** format. The **"know"** refers to the content whereas the **"do"** refers to a literacy standard and/or a higher-order thinking skill. The **"know"** portion of the objective should be leveraged to require students to ascend the pyramid of cognitive demand in order to: (1) build students understanding of a phenomenon; (2) connect the content to subsequent local, state, regional, national, or international happenings; and/or (3) solve a problem facing society.

SWBAT

IOT

Link to Literacy Standards: Content area teachers should be intentional about linking content instruction to one of the nine highly assessed informational literacy standards (even if its not prudent/appropriate to link the performance-based objective to an assessed literacy standards).

To which literacy standard(s) will instruction on this performance-based objective be linked?

Highly-Assessed Informational Literacy Standard	Select One or More (How will it/they be connected)?
Citing Textual Evidence	
Central Idea	
Summarizing	
Connections between Ideas, Individuals, and Events or Steps, Actions, and Events	
Unfamiliar Words & Phrases	

Highly-Assessed Informational Literacy Standard	Select One or More (How will it/they be connected)?
Text Structures	
Author's Point of View or Author's Purpose	
Author's Argument	
Drawing/Integrating Information from Multiple Sources	

General and Domain Specific Vocabulary Words:

List and operationally define key terms that are essential to student mastery of the performance-based objective. Students should be encouraged to use knowledge of Latin and Greek word parts and/or context clues to create meaning before and during reading.

What strategy(ies)/method(s) will be used to explicitly teach unfamiliar words, phrases, and symbols in the performance-based objective and in the primary and secondary sources to be used?

Consider annotating the primary and secondary sources.

Teacher Model: The teacher demonstrates what students should **know** and be **able to do** while students listen attentively, taking notes where appropriate.

Q1: What primary and/or secondary will be used to model the skill? List each primary and secondary source to be used in the teacher model and note the portion of the source(s) to be used if applicable.

Q2: Do the primary/secondary sources used in the teacher model reflect intentional/strategic exposure to a variety of sources? How so?

Q3: What is the plan for exposing students to a rich and rigorous evidence-based conversation and a model of composition (writing to inform; writing to explain; or constructing a viable argument and critiquing the reasoning of others, including the acknowledgement of the counterclaim) during the model? **Suggestion:** Consider the literacy graphic organizers for social studies.

Guided Practice: Students are asked to demonstrate developing knowledge of the objective by demonstrating their knowledge and ability in the large group setting. The teacher uses this opportunity to assess as many students as possible with special attention to struggling learners. This text/portion of the text can be written at the **instructional reading level** (grade level), since access to the text will be supported by the teacher. *If students are unsuccessful at this phase, then students would benefit from another teacher model.*

Q1: What primary and/or secondary will be used to engage students in guided practice? List each primary and secondary source to be used throughout guided practice and note the portion of the source(s) to be used if applicable.

Q2: Do the primary/secondary sources used throughout guided practice reflect intentional/strategic exposure to a variety of sources? How so?

Q3: What is the plan for exposing students to a rich and rigorous evidence-based conversation and a model of composition (writing to inform; writing to explain; or constructing a viable argument and critiquing the reasoning of others, including the acknowledgement of the counterclaim) throughout guided practice opportunities? **Suggestion:** Consider the literacy graphic organizers for social studies.

Collaborative Practice: Students are asked to work in groups of two to demonstrate developing knowledge of the objective. The teacher uses this opportunity to circulate the room assessing and assisting as many students as possible with special attention to struggling learners. This text/portion of the text should be written at the **independent level,** since students will be reading most of it without the teacher. *If students are successful in this phase, they are ready for the next step in the gradual release process.*

Q1: What primary and/or secondary will be used to engage students in collaborative practice? List each primary and secondary source to engage students in collaborative practice and note the portion of the source(s) to be used if applicable.

Q2: Do the primary/secondary sources used for collaborative practice reflect intentional/strategic exposure to a variety of sources? How so?

Q3: What is the plan for requiring students to engage in a rich and rigorous evidence-based conversation and co-composition (writing to inform; writing to explain; or constructing a viable argument and critiquing the reasoning of others, including the acknowledgement of the counterclaim) throughout guided practice opportunities? **Suggestion:** Consider the literacy graphic organizers for social studies.

Independent Practice: Students are asked to work independently to demonstrate knowledge of the objective. The teacher uses this opportunity to determine what students know and can do **without any assistance** from the teacher, teacher assistant, or peer. *If students are unsuccessful in this phase, then students may benefit from exposure to the general and domain specific vocabulary and/or exposure to a second round of the gradual release process.*

Q1: What primary and/or secondary will be used to provide students with an opportunity to practice independently? List each primary and secondary source to engage students in independent practice and note the portion of the source(s) to be used if applicable.

Q2: Do the primary/secondary sources used for independent practice reflect intentional/strategic exposure to a variety of sources? How so?

Q3: What is the plan for assessing **individual** students' ability to engage in a rich and rigorous evidence-based conversation and compose an original response to a **standards-related writing prompt** (writing to inform; writing to explain; or constructing a viable argument and critiquing the reasoning of others, including the acknowledgement of the counterclaim) **Suggestion:** Consider the literacy graphic organizers for social studies.

Homework for Students Struggling with this Performance-Based Objective: (Students would benefit from homework aligned with the prerequisite skill necessary to demonstrate mastery of the know and do objective).

Homework for Students Not Struggling with this Performance-Based Objective: (Non- struggling students would benefit from homework designed to enrich their ability to apply knowledge and skills aligned with the know and do objective).

Designing Performance-Based Instruction Aligned with the State Standards for Science

Number of Days Needed to Teach to Mastery:

State Standard under Study:

Performance-Based Objective: (Performance-Based Objectives should be composed in the **know and do** format. The **"know"** refers to the content whereas the **"do"** refers to a literacy standard and/or a higher-order thinking skill. The **"know"** portion of the objective should be leveraged to require students to ascend the pyramid of cognitive demand (i.e., knowledge, understanding, application, analysis, synthesis, evaluation, creation).

SWBAT

IOT

Link to Literacy Standards: Content area teachers should be intentional about linking content instruction to one of the nine highly assessed informational literacy standards (even if its not prudent/appropriate to link the performance-based objective to an assessed literacy standards).

To which literacy standard(s) will instruction on this performance-based objective be linked?

Highly-Assessed Informational Literacy Standard	Select One or More (How will it/they be connected)?
Citing Textual Evidence	
Central Idea	
Summarizing	
Connections between Ideas, Individuals, and Events or Steps, Actions, and Events	
Unfamiliar Words & Phrases	
Text Structures	
Author's Point of View or Author's Purpose	
Author's Argument	
Drawing/Integrating Information from Multiple Sources	

General and Domain Specific Vocabulary Words:

List and operationally define key terms that are essential to student mastery of the performance-based objective. Students should be encouraged to use knowledge of Latin and Greek word parts and/or context clues to create meaning before and during reading.

What strategy(ies)/method(s) will be used to explicitly teach unfamiliar words, phrases, and symbols in the performance-based objective and content-related texts? Consider annotating the performance-based objective and any content related text to be used to the teach concept(s) and skill(s) to mastery.

Engage: Each *lesson progression* should begin with a real-world hook that mentally engages students (an activity or question). The engagement activity or question is designed to: (1) capture student interest; (2) provide an opportunity for students to express what they know about the concept or skill being developed; and (3) facilitate connections between what students already know and the new concept under study/skill to be developed. Note the **engagement activity or question.** Be sure that it meets all three of the engagement criteria.

What is the plan for exposing students to a rich and rigorous evidence-based conversation and a model of composition (writing to inform; writing to explain; or constructing a viable argument and critiquing the reasoning of others) as a result of the **engagement** activity? **Suggestion:** Consider the literacy graphic organizers for science.

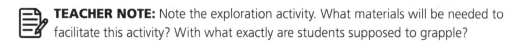 **TEACHER NOTE:** Which type of text (informative, explanatory, or opinion/argumentative) will students be required to compose to complete the engagement activity/respond to the engagement question? What rubric will be used to give students feedback on their response to the activity/question? Is it a school-wide or departmental rubric?

Explore/Guided Instruction: This phase is designed to provide students with an opportunity to carry out and hands-on activity through which they can explore the concept or skill being developed. Students should be a permitted to grapple with a content-related problem or phenomenon and describe it in their own words. This phase also allows students an opportunity to acquire a common set of experiences that they can use to aid themselves and assist their peers with making sense of the new concept or skill being developed.

 TEACHER NOTE: Note the exploration activity. What materials will be needed to facilitate this activity? With what exactly are students supposed to grapple?

What is the plan for exposing students to a rich and rigorous evidence-based conversation and a model of co-composition (writing to inform; writing to explain; or constructing a viable argument and critiquing the reasoning of others, during the **exploration** activity? **Suggestion:** Consider the literacy graphic organizers for science.

TEACHER NOTE: Which type of text (informative, explanatory, or opinion/ argumentative) will students be required to compose to complete the exploration/ guided instruction activity? What rubric will be used to give students feedback on their writing? Is it a school-wide or departmental rubric?

Explain/(Modeling with Science): After students have had an opportunity to explore the concept or skill being developed, the teacher should provide an explanation of the concept or phenomenon under study and/or an expert-level demonstration of the skill being developed to using the content-specific terms and/ or students should be required to provide the teacher with an explanation off the concept or phenomenon under study and/or a developing-level understanding of the skills being developed using the content-specific terms. The significant aspect of this phase is that explanation follows experience/exploration.

TEACHER NOTE: Script the teacher's explanation with sensitivity to gaps in students' content knowledge and common misconceptions. What material will be needed to facilitate this activity? If the teacher decides to allow students to facilitate the explanation, the teacher should be prepared to record student misconceptions and use them as teachable moment when they arise. Students must be required to use the language of the content throughout their explanation.

What is the plan for exposing students to a rich and rigorous evidence-based conversation and a model of composition (writing to inform; writing to explain; or constructing a viable argument and critiquing the reasoning of others, during the **explanation** activity? **Suggestion:** Consider the literacy graphic organizers for science.

TEACHER NOTE: Which type of text (informative, explanatory, or opinion/ argumentative) will students be required to compose to complete the explanation/ modeling with science activity? What rubric will be used to give students feedback on their writing? Is it a school-wide or departmental rubric?

Elaborate/(Collaborative Practice): This phase is designed to provide students with potentially multiple opportunities to apply what they have learned to new situations and by doing so, develop a deeper understanding of the concept/phenomenon or greater use of the skill being developed. It is important for students to be granted opportunities to discuss and compare their ideas with their peers during this phase. Flexible groups should be as small as possible/appropriate.

This phase is the final opportunity for the teacher to formatively assess student acquisition of new knowledge and skills prior to the final phase of instruction (the evaluation/independent practice phase). The teacher should therefore, use this phase to circulate the room assessing and assisting as many students as possible with special attention to struggling learners.

TEACHER NOTE: Note the elaboration activity(ies). (Be sure to plan and note more than one, as students may need additional practice). Be sensitive to student ability levels, special needs (accommodations and modifications), and English language proficiency. What materials will be needed to facilitate this activity?

What is the plan for exposing students to a rich and rigorous evidence-based conversation and co-composition (writing to inform; writing to explain; or constructing a viable argument and critiquing the reasoning of others, during the **elaboration** activity? **Suggestion:** Consider the literacy graphic organizers for science.

TEACHER NOTE: Which type of text (informative, explanatory, or opinion/ argumentative) will students be required to compose to complete the elaboration/ collaborative activity? What rubric will be used to give students feedback on their writing? Is it a school-wide or departmental rubric?

Evaluate (Independent Practice): The final phase is designed to provide an opportunity for students to: (1) demonstrate mastery; and (2) review and reflect on their own learning and new understanding and skills. Students should be required to provide evidence for changes to their understanding, skills, and beliefs (where appropriate).

TEACHER NOTE: Note the independent activity(ies). (Be sure to plan and note more than one, as students may need additional practice). Be sensitive to student ability levels, special needs (accommodations and modifications), and English language proficiency. What materials will be needed to facilitate this activity? How can interactive notebooks be incorporated to teach/reinforce "note taking" and "note keeping" skills?

What is the plan for exposing students to a rich and rigorous evidence-based conversation and independent composition (writing to inform; writing to explain; or constructing a viable argument and critiquing the reasoning of others, during the evaluation activity? Suggestion: Consider the literacy graphic organizers for science.

TEACHER NOTE: Which type of text (informative, explanatory, or opinion/argumentative) will students be required to compose to complete the evaluation/independent activity? What rubric will be used to give students feedback on their writing? Is it a school-wide or departmental rubric?

Homework for Students Struggling with this Performance-Based Objective: (Students would benefit from homework aligned with the prerequisite skill necessary to demonstrate mastery of the know and do objective).

Homework for Students Not Struggling with this Performance-Based Objective: (Non- struggling students would benefit from homework designed to enrich their ability to apply knowledge and skills aligned with the know and do objective).

Designing Performance-Based Instruction Aligned with the State Standards for Mathematics

Number of Days Needed to Teach to Mastery:

State Standard under Study:

Performance-Based Objective: (Performance-Based Objectives are composed in the know and do format. The "know" refers to the content whereas the "do" refers to a higher-order thinking skill and/or worthwhile mathematical task).

SWBAT

IOT

Link to Literacy Standards: Content area teachers should be intentional about linking content instruction to one of the nine highly assessed informational literacy standards (even if its not prudent/appropriate to link the performance-based objective to an assessed literacy standards).

To which literacy standard(s) will instruction on this performance-based objective be linked?

Coherence: How is this lesson connected to a previously mastered concept within this unit of study or from a previously taught unit of study?

Manipulatives: Which manipulatives will be used throughout the gradual release process to develop and assess students' conceptual understanding of abstract mathematical concept(s)?

General and Domain Specific Vocabulary Words:

List and operationally define key terms and/or symbols that are essential to student mastery of the objective. (Students should be encouraged to use knowledge of Latin and Greek word parts to develop a conceptual understanding of the concept under study).

What strategy(ies)/method(s) will be used to explicitly teach unfamiliar words, phrases, and symbols in the performance-based objective and practice problems?

Teacher Model: The teacher demonstrates what students should **know** and **be able to do** while students listen attentively, taking notes where appropriate.

What real-world problems (worthwhile mathematical tasks) will be used by the teacher to model skills /demonstrate application of mathematical concept(s)?

TEACHER NOTE: Consider working each problem in advance of instruction to gain firsthand experience with the nuances of each question with attention to your thought processes and probable misconceptions.

Guided Practice: Students are asked to demonstrate developing knowledge of the performance-based objective by demonstrating their knowledge and ability in the large group setting. The teacher uses this opportunity to assess as many students as possible with special attention to struggling learners. *If students are unsuccessful at this phase, then students would benefit from another teacher model.*

What real-world problems (worthwhile mathematical tasks) will be presented to students in order to provide students with multiple opportunities to apply their knowledge of mathematical concepts through guided practice?

TEACHER NOTE: Consider working each problem in advance of instruction to gain firsthand experience with the nuances of each question with attention to your thought processes and probable misconceptions.

How will the teacher know what **each student knows and can do** during the guided practice opportunity? How will students be assessed through writing and speaking?

Collaborative Practice: Students are asked to work in groups of two to demonstrate developing knowledge of the objective. The teacher uses this opportunity to circulate the room assessing and assisting as many students as possible with special attention to struggling learners. *If students are successful in this phase, they are ready for the next step in the gradual release process.*

What real-world problems (worthwhile mathematical tasks) will be presented to students in order to provide students with multiple opportunities (with a partner) to apply their knowledge of mathematical concepts?

TEACHER NOTE: Consider working each problem in advance of instruction to gain firsthand experience with the nuances of each question with attention to your thought processes and probable misconceptions.

How will the teacher know what **each student knows and can do** during the collaborative practice opportunity? How can students be assessed through writing and speaking?

Independent Practice: Students are asked to work independently to demonstrate knowledge of the objective. The teacher uses this opportunity to determine what students know and can do without any assistance from the teacher, teacher assistant, or peer. *If students are unsuccessful in this phase, then students may benefit from exposure to the general and domain specific vocabulary and/or exposure to a second round of the gradual release process.*

What real-world problems (worthwhile mathematical tasks) will be presented to students in order to provide students with multiple opportunities (without any assistance) to apply their knowledge of mathematical concepts?

TEACHER NOTE: Consider working each problem in advance of instruction to gain firsthand experience with the nuances of each question with attention to your thought processes and probable misconceptions.

Will students be able to use manipulatives during independent practice to demonstrate mastery of abstract mathematical concepts? If so, which students and why?

Homework for Students Struggling with this Performance-Based Objective: (Students would benefit from homework aligned with the prerequisite skill necessary to demonstrate mastery of the know and do objective).

Homework for Students Not Struggling with this Performance-Based Objective: (Non- struggling students would benefit from homework designed to enrich their ability to apply knowledge and skills aligned with the know and do objective).

CHAPTER SEVEN

Develop an Action Plan for the Tested Areas and Report the Progress

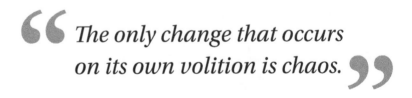

The only change that occurs on its own volition is chaos.

If you will recall in chapter 2, I suggested that schools develop an Action Plan for English/Language Arts and Mathematics. Remember, your school-wide, cluster-wide, or district-wide action plan is designed to explicitly teach and assess students' knowledge of a subset of standards-based skills that will be appear on the end-of-grade and/or end-of-course assessments for the tested grades in English/Language Arts and Mathematics. The Action Plan simply consists of a series of 5-question pre-tests (short cycle assessments) followed by targeted instruction on the focus skill for just a few minutes a day at the beginning of a designated number of periods/blocks, followed by an end-of-the-week administration of the same quiz that students were given at the top of the week (the pre-test and the post-test are the same exact quiz).

The Action plan is designed to give teachers and administrators real-time data on 10–15 skills derived from broad standards that we know will be tested on the interim/assessments throughout the year and ultimately the end-of-grade and/or end-of-course assessments. The skills that are taught and assessed through the Action Plan must not exceed the demands of the grade-level standard; that's why I refer to assessment limits at the ceiling. Assessment limits represent the most that will be assessed relative to a given standard and by default, becomes the very least that should be assessed. If an assessment limit exists for a particular standards-based skill, it will be evident in the standard.

After using the demands of the state standards for English/Language Arts and Mathematics for each tested grade, select the 10–15 skills/assessment limits upon which your action plan will focus. Once you have identified the skills, construct an action plan calendar and assign each skill to a week [or two—you choose] of the school year that precede the end-of-course and/or end-of-grade assessments. By teaching the skills derived from the standards explicitly, you are directly exposing your student body to the state assessment one tiny skill at a time. Regardless of the level of your school (elementary, middle, or high), the following features of the Integrated Approach Action Plan noted on the next page are universal and should be implemented with fidelity for optimal gains.

Table 7.1—Universal Integrated Approach Action Plan Elements

☐ **Approximately 5–7 minutes of instruction on the skill** of the week becomes the drill prior to beginning your regularly scheduled instruction. This practice only applies to the days on which you are not pre-testing or post-testing.

☐ **The 5-question, multiple choice pre-test** on the skill must be administered on the first day of the week prior to instruction on the skill of the week and the same 5-question post-test must be administered on the **final day of the week** to assess student acquisition of the skill. If you have short weeks in the calendar, you may wish to teach a skill that week without assessing it or combine a short week with a 5-day week to have an 8-day week to teach and assess a conceptually difficult skill. Educational Epiphany can supply you with theses assessments or you can compose your own. But be careful, they must be aligned properly.

☐ **The pre-test is the post-test** (same questions). You may change the order of the questions if you think students will attempt to memorize the order of the questions.

☐ Teachers should **refrain from** reviewing the questions on the pre-test; doing so will invalidate the post-test results at the end of the week.

☐ Use your state curriculum glossary of terms or other resources to phrase the questions on the pre-test/post-test so students become accustomed to the academic language.

☐ Use a teach timer to ensure that teachers refrain from using excessive instructional time on the skill drill at the top of the class; 5–7 minutes should be sufficient. It just depends upon the skill. But if teachers can teach the skill in two minutes, even better.

☐ Use a short-form scantron for students to record their responses to the pre-test/post-test; it is easy to grade. The size of your staff will dictate the number of scantron machines you will need to buy/lease and the size of your student body will dictate the number of scantrons you will need to purchase. If you have advanced grading technology, use that instead of the scantrons. Please **do not allow** a student to grade another student's pre-test/post-test; it will invalidate the data. You must be able to trust the data.

☐ Record the post-test grade in the grade book. Students should be held accountable for their score on the post-test.

☐ **If a student is absent for the pre-test,** do not require them to take it upon their return, just mark an "A" for absent in the spreadsheet. I will come back to this later in this chapter.

☐ **If a student is absent for the post-test,** they must take it upon their return; you will need their score for the spreadsheet and grade book.

☐ Students will have demonstrated mastery of the skill if they score of 4 of 5 or 5 of 5. All students who scored a 0–3 should be required to take the post-test on the last day of the week.

☐ **Students who scored a 4 on the pre-test** should be allowed to take the post-test in order to attempt to earn a 5 of 5.

☐ The instructional leadership team should make every effort provide the faculty with materials to introduce each assessment limit to students (i.e., for "Prefix" week, each teacher should be given a list of prefixes, for "Making Inferences" week, each teacher should be provided with the graphic organizer to be used by all to teach the skill). Be sure that the materials that teachers are offered are 'aligned' to the skill.

 TEACHER NOTE: Your action plan will differ depending upon the grade level of your school (elementary, middle, or high school).

Elementary schools should do the following for optimal results:

1. Implement the plan in grades 3–5 only.

2. Because grade levels typically have different schedules and because elementary teachers are generalists (they teach all of the core subjects), decide which times of the day would lend themselves to the 5–7 minutes of skill-driven instruction. One elementary school that implemented and subsequently demonstrated the most significant gains in their state, decided to teach the assessment limits on the following schedule:

    a. In Homeroom (English/Language Arts Skill of the Week)

    b. Before Lunch (English/Language Arts Skill of the Week)

    c. After Lunch (Mathematics Skill of the Week)

    d. In Elective Course (English/Language Arts Skill of the Week)

    e. Last Subject of Day (Mathematics Assessment Limit of the Week)

3. Although the skills were taught three times per day in this example, students would only take one pre-test/post-test per week on the English/Language Arts skill and one pre-test/post-test per week on the Mathematics skill.

TEACHER NOTE: If your students struggle more with mathematics than reading then your team may decide to facilitate three opportunities for Mathematics skill instruction and only two opportunities for English/Language Arts.

Middle schools should adhere to the following for optimal gains:

1. Compose a set of five-question, multiple-choice pre-tests/posts for English/Language Arts; Mathematics; Literacy in Social Studies; Literacy in Science; and Literacy in the Technical Subjects (electives) for each grade [6–8].

2. The English/Language Arts skills should be taught and assessed in English/Language Arts, Social Studies, Science, and in Technical Subjects (So on the first day of the week, students will have four pre-tests and four on the last day of the week). It's ok. The quizzes should only take a few minutes. If they take longer than a few minutes, they are too complex. Stick to 5 questions. The pre-test/post-test should assess student knowledge of a standard-aligned skill using a text related to the content area that assesses the skill (i.e., The social studies pre-test/post-test should use social studies related texts and so forth).

3. The skills of week for Technical Subjects should be limited to skills like citing textual evidence, main topic/main idea/central idea, making inferences, summarizing, determining the meaning of unfamiliar words, text features and search tools, text structures, author's purpose, tone, author's argument, extracting information from multiple mediums and formats, and integrating information from multiple sources, depending upon the grade band. Why? These are the 'literacy' skills that students must be able to transfer to all informational-text reading opportunities. These skills, when we have them, make each of us 'literate.'

4. The literary (not to be conflated with literacy) skills should only be taught and assessed in the English/Language Arts courses using literary text. Simply combine the informational and literary text skills into one action plan. Be prepared to make a Sophie's choice.

5. The mathematics skills should only be taught and assessed in mathematics classes/blocks.

High schools should follow the following structures for optimal results:

1. Compose a set of five-question, multiple-choice pre-tests/posts for English/Language Arts; Mathematics; Literacy in Social Studies; Literacy in Science; and Literacy in the Technical Subjects (electives) for each grade [9–11 or 12]. You may consider exempting grade 12. They are typically not responsible for end-of-course or end-of-grade assessments.

2. The English/Language Arts skills should be taught and assessed in English/Language Arts, Social Studies, Science, and in Technical Subjects (So on the first day of the week, students will have four pre-tests and four on the last day of the week). It's ok. The quizzes should only take a few minutes. If they take longer than a few minutes, they are too complex. Remember,

stick to 5 questions. The pre-test/post-test should assess student knowledge of a standard-aligned skill using a text related to the content area that assesses the skill (i.e., The art pre-test/post-test should use a text the teacher might use to teach art).

3. The literary (not to be conflated with literacy) skills should only be taught and assessed in the English/Language Arts courses using literary text. Simply combine the informational and literary text skills into one action plan. Be prepared to make a Sophie's choice.

4. The skills of week for Technical Subjects should be limited to skills like citing textual evidence, main topic/main idea/central idea, making inferences, summarizing, determining the meaning of unfamiliar words, text features and search tools, text structures, author's purpose, tone, author's argument, extracting information from multiple mediums and formats, and integrating information from multiple sources, depending upon the grade band. Why? These are the 'literacy' skills that students must be able to transfer to all informational-text reading opportunities. These skills, when we have them, make each of us 'literate.'

5. The mathematics skills should only be taught and assessed in mathematics blocks/classes.

Regardless of your schools grade level, your instructional leadership team should facilitate professional development sessions to ensure that each teacher has expert-level knowledge of each action plan skill. This professional development should take place prior to requiring the faculty and staff to teach and assess student knowledge of the skills. In many cases, the instructional leaders will be learning along with the teachers and instructional assistants. This approach is not about PRIDE; rather it is about RESULTS. Your professional development must demystify the demands of each skill in order to ensure that students acquire attain mastery.

Below, you will find a sample Action Plan Calendar for English/Language Arts for a middle school.

Table 7.2—Sample Action Pan for Informational Text Standards (Middle School)

Skills	Week
Prefixes and Base Words	September 7
Suffixes	September 14
Vocabulary-in-Context	September 21
Text/Print Features	September 28
Graphic Aids	October 5
Informational Aids	October 12
Organizational Aids	October 19
Main Idea and Summarizing	October 26
Identifying Key Details	November 2
Fact and Opinion	November 9
Making Inferences	November 16
Drawing Conclusions *(Teach Only Skill-Short Week, No Pre-test/Post-test)*	November 23
Making Generalizations	November 30
Organizational Patterns Sequential & Chronological Order, Cause & Effect, Problem-Solution, Similarities & Differences Description, and Main Idea & Supporting Details	December 7

Skills	Week
Author's Purpose/Text Purpose	December 14
Author's Argument and Author's Tone *(Teach Only Skill-Short Week, No Pre-test/Post-test)*	December 21
Author's Viewpoint	January 4
Explaining how Organizational Patterns Supports Text Purpose	January 11
Paraphrasing *(Teach Only Skill-Short Week, No Pre-test/Post-test)*	January 18
Comparing and Contrasting	January 25
Idiomatic Expressions	February 1
Evaluating Fulfillment of Reading Purpose *(Teach Only Skill-Short Week, No Pre-test/Post-test)*	February 8
Connotation & Denotation	February 15
Analyzing the Reliability of Information	February 22
Critiquing the Reasoning of Others	March 1

Note: This chart is illustrative.

When I developed the Integrated Approach to Student Achievement nearly a decade ago in 2003, I had no idea that this element of the model would have such a profound impact on students, staff, and the bottom line. Students who have been unsuccessful academically have a heightened awareness of their shortcomings; they have anxiety about being in the classroom setting, and have fears about being singled-out as a low-performer. In ways unimaginable, this element of the approach addresses and rectifies a mammoth impediment to student achievement—student apathy.

Under this approach, I recommend that each classroom should have a highly-visible data center that allows students to track their performance on the pre-tests and post-tests each week in order to promote awareness of individual and class performance. Students should be taught how to use their individual performance to set academic goals for upcoming pre-tests and post-tests. They should be told that the weekly assessments actually are the state exam, one skill at a time [for English/Language Arts and Mathematics]. Moreover, students should be aware of the potential correlation between their performance on the pre-tests/post-tests and their subsequent performance on state mandated assessments. To that end, each week, students should be strongly encouraged to visit the data center in each of their classes.

One of the unintended, but promising outcomes of this approach is the response that students have to tracking their own personal performance. They revel in their success on the assessments, particularly those who had not previously experienced academic success. In many cases, learners who were formerly unmotivated and detached from instruction, race to the data center in each classroom to check their scores and celebrate their performance.

For a model Integrated Approach Data Center Progress-Monitoring Spreadsheet and an explanation of each component, see the next page.

Table 7.3—Data Center Progress-Monitoring Spreadsheet

Integrated Approach Informational Text Skill — Mr. Hamlin (Grade 6)

Student	Designation	A Score	Prefixes Pre Test	Prefixes Post Test	Suffixes Pre Test	Suffixes Post Test	Root Words Pre Test	Root Words Post Test	Vocabulary in Context Pre Test	Vocabulary in Context Post Test	Text Features Pre Test	Text Features Post Test	Main Idea Pre Test	Main Idea Post Test	Supporting Details Pre Test	Supporting Details Post Test	Fact and Opinion Pre Test	Fact and Opinion Post Test	Inferences Pre Test	Inferences Post Test
1	54484664 B	383	4	5	3	5														
2	6262616 A	435	3	4	2	4														
3	5151155 P	418	3	4	4	4														
4	51515151 B	383	2	3	4	4														
5	65151511 A	428	5	5	2	4														
6	26544155 P	403	4	4	0	3														
7	51515151 B	311	3	3	4	4														
8	51515151 A	424	5	5	2	4														
9	89416511 A	429	5	5	5	5														
10	51615154 P	414	2	4	3	4														
11	65265556 P	423	2	4	4	4														
12	51651511 P	424	2	4	2	4														
13	51519561 P	426	3	4	5	5														
14	65946516 B	310	4	4	1	4														
15	62654864 P	404	3	4	3	4														
16	96251516 P	409	3	2	5	3														
17	51616515 A	441	4	4	4	4														
18	61213156 A	458	3	4	2	4														
19	51654651 A	520	4	4	4	5														
20	65165150 B	335	3	4	5	5														
21	3260216 A	464	4	4	3	4	5													
22	0065646 A	541	5	5	5	5	4													
Number of Mastered			10	18	11	21	2	0	0	0	0	0	0	0	0	0	0	0	0	0
Number of Non-Mastered			12	4	11	1	0	0	0	0	0	0	0	0	0	0	0	0	0	0
Perent Mastered			45%	82%	50%	4.8%	95%	100%	0%	0%	0%	0%	0%	0%	0%	0%	0%	0%	0%	0%

NOTE: It may be useful to use this spreadsheet at parent-teacher conferences to apprise parents of their child's progress.

Each progress-monitoring spreadsheet contains the following:

- A confidential student identification number (refrain from using students' names),

- Performance level (on the previous year's state assessment—i.e., below basic, basic, proficient, advanced),

- Scale score (on previous year's state assessment),

- Pre-test score column for each skill to be taught and assessed,

- Post-test score column for each skill to be taught and assessed, and

- Formulas embedded in the spreadsheet that calculate,

- Number of students who scored 80% or better on the pre-test,

- Number of students who did not score 80% or better on the post-test, and

- Percentage of students who mastered the pre-test and post-test.

Elementary Schools:

1. Since elementary teachers teach every core subject to the same students each day (for the most part) teachers in grades 3–5 will need one progress-monitoring spreadsheet for the English/Language Arts skills and one progress-monitoring spreadsheet for the mathematics skills to be covered. Remember, even though it is recommended that teachers teach the skill of the week 2 or 3 times a day, teachers will only compose/procure one pre-test/post-test for each skill in your grade level.

   a. The informational text/literary text skill progress-monitoring spreadsheet should have students' level of performance and scale score from the previous year's English/Language Arts state assessment.

   b. The mathematics skill progress-monitoring spreadsheet should have students' level of performance and scale score from the previous years' mathematics state assessment.

2. Technical Subjects teachers will just need one progress-monitoring spreadsheet representing 10 informational text standards-based skills for each class that they teach. The 10 skills should be the same no matter the technical subjects class. Remember, each Technical Subjects teacher will administer their own Literacy in the Technical Subjects pre-test/post-test for each of the 10 skills that they will cover.

Middle and High Schools

1. Since most middle school teachers teach one subject to the same students each day. Teachers in grades 6–8 and 9–11 will need one progress-monitoring spreadsheet for each class populated with the skills to be covered.

2. Technical Subjects teachers will just need one progress-monitoring spreadsheet representing 10 informational text standard-based skills for each class that they teach. The 10 skills should be the same no matter the technical subjects class. Remember each Technical subjects teacher will administer their own Literacy in the Technical Subjects pre-test/post-test for each of the 10 skills that they will cover.

3. The English/Language Arts, Literacy in Social Studies, Literacy in Science, and Literacy in Technical Subjects skill progress-monitoring spreadsheet should have students' level of performance and scale score from the previous year's English/Language Arts state assessment.

4. The Mathematics skill progress-monitoring spreadsheet should have students' level of performance and scale score from the previous years' mathematics state assessment.

TEACHER NOTE: Teachers are urged to use pre-test/post-test data to assign homework, create vacation review-packets, to guide their parent-teacher conference conversations and re-teaching decisions.

In addition to reporting data for students, student performance on the pre-tests/post-tests should be published for the faculty and staff. At each monthly faculty meeting, grade level meeting, or content area meeting, it is prudent to share the performance of students on the pre-tests/post-tests. Sharing the data in this incremental manner creates enormous momentum and buy-in for the approach and allows teachers to see the impact of explicitly exposing students to the skills each week. You will need to merge the data from each of the spreadsheets for each grade 3, 4, and 5 (elementary schools). This is beneficial to the teachers in each grade because it reveals students' strengths and weaknesses on each skill by grade. A similar practice is recommended for the middle and high schools. It is recommended that skill-data be reported by each subject area, rather than by grade. This practice allows each content area, including Technical Subjects to contemplate the impact of their contribution on student acquisition of new skills.

Do this each month to keep the staff motivated. Remember, the skills are the state assessment presented in small pieces, one each week of the school year [for English/Language Arts and Mathematics] and infusing the literacy skills in to the other content areas will accelerate transdisciplinary literacy and student achievement. Teachers and school leaders can even use this data to predict student performance on the state assessment. Gains on the pre-tests/post-test will invariably translate into gains on the state assessment. Below are sample monthly data reporting charts described above.

Table 7.4—Integrated Approach Monthly 4-Skill Reporting

September English/Language Arts Skills—Grade 4

Grade 4	Proficient on Pre-Test	Proficient on Post-Test	Gain
Prefixes	39%	89%	50%
Suffixes	25%	81%	56%
Base Words	41%	92%	51%
Vocabulary-in-Context	36%	74%	38%

TEACHER NOTE: Students will be amazed with the level of gains that your students will make after just three days of instruction on the skills. You may even wish to report this data to parents at monthly PTA meetings.

Table 7.5—Integrated Approach Monthly 4-Skill Reporting Chart (Middle and High)

November Informational Text Skills—Social Studies Classes

Grade 4	Proficient on Pre-Test	Proficient on Post-Test	Gain
Making Inferences	24%	78%	54%
Summarizing	19%	65%	46%
Author's Purpose	20%	82%	62%
Text Structures	24%	54%	30%

TEACHER NOTE: There was a 62% gain in students' ability to determine author's purpose. How might they have performed relative to this skill without exposure through the action plan?

Table 7.6—Integrated Approach Monthly 4-Skill Reporting Chart (Elementary)

September Math Assessment Limits—Grade 3

Grade 3	Proficient on Pre-Test	Proficient on Post-Test	Gain
Multiplying Whole Numbers	54%	88%	34%
Dividing Whole Numbers	25%	65%	40%
Adding/Subtracting Fractions	18%	45%	27%
Multiplying Fractions and Mixed Numbers	9%	42%	33%

TEACHER NOTE: The data indicates that grade 3 student made significant gains on adding/subtracting fractions and multiplying fractions and mixed numbers, but the is still a great deal of work to be done on those skills. The point of celebration however, should not be diminished; there was a 27% and 33% gain in student understanding of these skills respectively.

Table 7.7—Integrated Approach Monthly 4-Skill Reporting Chart (Middle and High)

February Mathematics Skills—Mathematics Classes

Grade 6	Proficient on Pre-Test	Proficient on Post-Test	Gain
Setting up Ratios	44%	69%	25%
Determining Unit Rate	35%	71%	36%
Evaluating Expressions	14%	56%	42%
Finding the Area of Composite Figures	2%	24%	22%

TEACHER NOTE: Perhaps teachers need to examine their approach to teaching finding the area of composite figures. Students did not respond well to the instruction that they received.

Author's Reflection

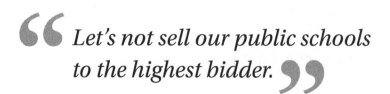 *Let's not sell our public schools to the highest bidder.*

As I wrap up this conversation with you, my conscientious colleagues, I want to share a few, final thoughts. School closures and school consolidations are not tools for reform or school/district improvement. In actuality, and in many cases, school closures and consolidations are an act of fear. Don't close our public schools. Don't close our neighborhood schools. Instead, make them better ensuring that students have equitable access to instruction of the highest quality. That's reform America!

I want to thank each of you who support my work across the nation. Likewise, I would like to thank each of you for selecting this book as a tool to assist you on your journey toward heightened student outcomes and school improvement. It is my hope that your careful exploration of the content of this book will result in children having even greater access to schooling experiences of the highest quality. This text is not intended to be a script followed to the letter, rather a toolkit of proven ideas and practices designed for practitioners by a practitioner. Implement all or some of the ideas presented in the text, but I implore you to refrain from implementing everything in one fell swoop. I am not a proponent of an 'everything-first' approach to implementation. Process and discuss the content of each chapter with your team and develop a thoughtful plan for change.

And yes, I am well aware that there is a weighty imperative on teachers, school leaders, and central office personnel to improve student achievement right away, but remember, it's the people—our greatest resource to children—who will be tasked with implementation. Be careful not to burn them out. Find your implementation sweet-spot and execute change at a rate that is sensitive to human dignity and reflective of mutual respect.

You may have asked yourself at some point while reading this text, "How did the name Integrated Approach to Student Achievement come about?" Here's how.

We have made student achievement and school improvement such an arduous task, but it doesn't have to be. From coast to coast, schools and districts are being managed and operated like start-ups—with disjointed, disparate expectations, systems, and structures. Yet, we simultaneously hope for improvements in student achievement. We need more than hope as a strategy to improve student achievement. Schools and districts must blend into one unified whole, ensuring that each part (i.e., team, grade level, content area, school-based leadership team, cluster of schools, district-level department, senior leadership) is working together in an integrated way to promote the same outcome…student achievement.

When teachers, school leaders, and central office personnel who support schools authentically become members of the same culture of instruction—a culture that insists upon methodical alignment of curriculum, instruction, and assessment or what I refer to as strategic integration of common instructional knowledge, common instructional language, and common instructional tools—then and only will the alchemy of student achievement become the resultant byproduct.

In the absence of an integrated approach to setting and managing expectations, building content knowledge, calibrating practices, and supporting the classroom (the unit of change) there will be no transformation. It's just that simple.

Our students and families are counting on us to figure it out. Zip code cannot remain a determinant of student achievement. We can and must do this. It is our moral imperative. The content of this text is irrespective of state lines and state standards. This text will assist school-based, district-level, and state-level teams; teacher and school administrator education programs; school board associations; and professional organizations to not only speak the same language—the language of student achievement and school improvement—but implement coherent research-driven strategies that bring certainty to the calamity that is all too often a part of our experience as public educators. **172**

Instructional leaders, you must lead instructionally. To do this work at the intensity that children and families deserve, we must be instructionally informed so that we can successfully address any threat to student achievement. You must become an authority of curriculum and instruction—a connoisseur.

Lastly, my final appeal, though arguably emotional, it has its origin in the depths of my soul.

Help children.

Bibliography

Baker, J. A. (1999). Teacher-student interaction in urban at-risk classrooms: Differentiated behavior, relationship quality, and student satisfaction with school. *The Elementary School Journal*, 100, 57–70.

Bloom, B. S. (1956). *Taxonomy of educational objectives, the classification of educational goals-handbook*. New York, NY: McKay.

Brown, K. E. & Medway, F. J. (2007). School climate and teacher beliefs in a school effectively serving poor South Carolina (USA) African America students: A case study. *Teaching and Teacher Education*, 23, 529–540.

Delpit, L. (2006). *Other people's children: Cultural conflict in the classroom*. New York, NY: The New Press.

Dickey, D. (2016). The African American middle school male achievement gap and performance on state assessments. *George Washington University–Educational Administration and Policy Studies*. George Washington University. ProQuest UMI.

Eisner, E. (1979). The educational imagination. On the design and evaluation of school programs. Upper Saddle River, NJ: Merrill Prentice Hall.

Fisher, E. J. (2005). Black student achievement and the oppositional culture model. *The Journal of Negro Education*, 74, 201–209.

Goddard, R. D., Hoy, W. K., & Hoy, A. W. (2000). Collective teacher efficacy: Its meaning, measure, and impact on student achievement. *American Educational Research Journal*, 37 (2), 479–507.

Hudley, C. A. (1997). Teaceher practices and student motivation in a middle school program for African American males. *Urban Education*, 32, 304–319.

Newmann, F. M., Byrk, A. S., & Nagoaka, J. K. (2001) *Authentic intellectual work and standardized tests: Conflict or coexistence? Improving Chicago's schools*. Chicago, IL: Consortium on Chicago Schools Research.

Patterson, K. B. (2005). Increasing outcomes for African American males in special education with the use of guided notes. *Journal of Negro Education*, 74, 311–320.

Quinn, M. M. (2002). Changing antisocial behavior patterns in young boys: A structured cooperative learning approach. *Education and Treatment of Children*, 25, 36.

Wilson, G. L., & Michaels, C. A. (2006). General and special education students' perceptions of co-teaching: Implications for secondary-level literacy instruction, *Reading and Writing Quarterly*, 22, 205–225.

Appendix

Educational Epiphany Next Generation Graphic Organizers Excerpt for Reading Informational Text Standards

Standard: RI2 for Grades Kindergarten—Grade 12

Educational Epiphany Next Generation Graphic Organizers Excerpt for Mathematics

Operations and Algebraic Thinking—Grade 3

Numbers in Operations in Base Ten—Grade 5

Statistics and Probability—Grade 7

RI K.2
With prompting and support, identify the main topic and retell the key details of a text

Topic (subject):

Key detail that supports the topic:

Key detail that supports the topic:

Key detail that supports the topic:

Key detail that supports the topic:

Key detail that supports the topic:

Key detail that supports the topic:

www.educationalepiphany.com | 410-258-6443

Identify the main topic and retell the key details of a text

Title of text:

Author of text:

Main topic (subject) of text:

Retell a key detail (important words or phrases) **that supports the main topic** (subject) **of the text:**

Retell a key detail (important words or phrases) **that supports the main topic** (subject) **of the text:**

Retell a key detail (important words or phrases) **that supports the main topic** (subject) **of the text:**

Retell a key detail (important words or phrases) **that supports the main topic** (subject) **of the text:**

Retell a key detail (important words or phrases) **that supports the main topic** (subject) **of the text:**

RI 2.2a
Identify the main topic of a multiparagraph text as well as the focus of specific paragraphs within the text

Title of text:

Author of text:

Main topic (subject) of text:

Key detail (important words or phrases) that supports **the main topic** (subject) of the text:

Key detail (important words or phrases) that supports **the main topic** (subject) of the text:

Key detail (important words or phrases) that supports **the main topic** (subject) of the text:

Key detail (important words or phrases) that supports **the main topic** (subject) of the text:

Key detail (important words or phrases) that supports **the main topic** (subject) of the text:

Key detail (important words or phrases) that supports **the main topic** (subject) of the text:

RI 2.2b
Identify the main topic of a multiparagraph text as well as the focus of specific paragraphs within the text

Title of text:

Author of text:

Main topic (subject) of text:

Key detail (important words or phrases) **that supports the main topic** (subject) **of the text** in paragraph 1:

Key detail (important words or phrases) **that supports the main topic** (subject) **of the text** in paragraph 2:

Key detail (important words or phrases) **that supports the main topic** (subject) **of the text** in paragraph 3:

Key detail (important words or phrases) **that supports the main topic** (subject) **of the text** in paragraph 4:

RI 2.2c
Identify the main topic of a multiparagraph text as well as the focus of specific paragraphs within the text

Title of text:

Author of text:

Main topic (subject) of text:

Key detail (important words or phrases) **that supports the main topic** (subject) **of the text** in paragraph 5:

Key detail (important words or phrases) **that supports the main topic** (subject) **of the text** in paragraph 6:

Key detail (important words or phrases) **that supports the main topic** (subject) **of the text** in paragraph 7:

Key detail (important words or phrases) **that supports the main topic** (subject) **of the text** in paragraph 8:

Determining the main idea of a text; recounting key details and explaining how they support the main idea

Topic:

Main idea:

Key detail:

Key detail:

Key detail:

Explanation of how key details support the main idea:

Determining the main idea of a text and explaining how it is supported by key details; summarize the text

Topic:

Main idea:

Key detail:

Key detail:

Key detail:

Explanation of how key details support the main idea:

EPIPHANY WORD BANK

Explanation– a statement that makes something clear

Key details– important words or phrases

Main idea– what the text is mostly about

Support– hold up or serve as a foundation

Topic– the subject of the text

RI 4.2b
Determining the main idea of a text and explaining how it is supported by key details; summarize the text

Topic:

Main idea of text:

Key detail:

Key detail:

Key detail:

Summary of text with references to key details:

RI 4.2c
Determining the main idea of a text and explaining how it is supported by key details; summarize the text

Summary (including references to key details):

RI 5.2
Determining two or more main ideas of a text and explaining how they are supported by key ideas; summarizing the text

Topic:

Key details– important words or phrases

Main idea– what the text is mostly about

Summary– a brief statement that contains the essential ideas of a longer passage

Support– hold up or serve as a foundation

Topic– the subject of the text

Main idea:

Main idea:

Key detail:

Key detail:

Key detail:

Key detail:

Explanation of how key details support the main idea:

Explanation of how key details support the main idea:

Summary of the text:

RI 6.2
Determining the central idea of a text and how it is conveyed through particular details and providing a summary distinct from personal opinions or judgments

Title of text:	Topic (subject) of text:

Central idea 1:

Detail that supports the central idea	
Detail that supports the central idea	
Detail that supports the central idea	
Detail that supports the central idea	

Summary of the text (distinct from personal opinions or judgments):

EPIPHANY WORD BANK

Central idea– the concept, thought, notion, or impression that is of greatest importance in the text or in a portion of the text; it may be implied or explicitly stated
Convey– to communicate or make known
Distinct– separate or different from
Summary– a brief statement that contains the essential ideas of a longer passage
Opinion– a belief or conclusion held with confidence, but not substantiated proof
Judgment– an informed and objective opinion formulated without bias
Topic– subject

Determining two or more central ideas in a text and analyzing their development over the course of the text; providing an objective summary of the text

Title of text:

Central idea 1:

Detail that supports the central idea	
Detail that supports the central idea	
Detail that supports the central idea	
Detail that supports the central idea	

Title of text:

Central idea 2:

Detail that supports the central idea	
Detail that supports the central idea	
Detail that supports the central idea	
Detail that supports the central idea	

Title of text:

3,Central idea 1:

Detail that supports the central idea	
Detail that supports the central idea	
Detail that supports the central idea	
Detail that supports the central idea	

EPIPHANY WORD BANK

Analyze– to break into smaller components to study or examine

Central idea– the concept, thought, notion, or impression that is of greatest importance in the text or in a portion of the text; it may be implied or explicitly stated

Objective– not influenced by personal feelings or opinions in considering and representing facts

Summary– a brief statement that contains the essential ideas of a longer passage

www.educationalepiphany.com | 410-258-6443

187

RI 7.2b

Determining two or more central ideas in a text and analyzing their development over the course of the text; providing an objective summary of the text

Central idea 1:	Central idea 2:	Central idea 3:
Detail that supports the introduction of central idea 1:	Detail that supports the introduction of central idea 2:	Detail that supports the introduction of central idea 3:
Detail that supports the development of central idea 1:	Detail that supports the development of central idea 2:	Detail that supports the development of central idea 3:
Detail that supports the refinement of central idea 1:	Detail that supports the refinement of central idea 2:	Detail that supports the refinement of central idea 3:

Details that support the **introduction** of the central idea

Details that support the **development** of the central idea

Details that support the **refinement** of the central idea

© Educational Epiphany

EPIPHANY WORD BANK

Analyze– to break into smaller components and study or examine

Central idea– the concept, thought, notion, or impression that is of greatest importance in the text or in a portion of the text; it may be implied or explicitly stated

Introduce– the act of providing (someone) with beginning knowledge or first experience with something

Develop– to cause to grow and become more mature, advanced, or elaborate

Objective– not influenced by personal feelings or opinions in considering and representing facts

Refine– to improve by making small changes

www.educationalepiphany.com | 410-258-6443

RI 7.2c
Determining two or more central ideas in a text and analyzing their development over the course of the text; providing an objective summary of the text

Use the details that support the central ideas to objectively summarize the text.

RI 8.2a
Determining a central idea of a text and analyzing its development over the course of the text, including its relationship to supporting ideas; providing an objective summary of the text

Central idea:

Detail that develops the central idea:	Explanation of relationship between detail(s) and the central idea:
Detail that develops the central idea:	Explanation of relationship between detail(s) and the central idea:
Detail that develops the central idea:	Explanation of relationship between detail(s) and the central idea:
Detail that develops the central idea:	Explanation of relationship between detail(s) and the central idea:

EPIPHANY WORD BANK

Key details– important words or phrases
Main idea– what the text is mostly about
Reference– mention
Summary– a brief statement that contains the essential ideas of a longer passage

RI 8.2b
Determining a central idea of a text and analyzing its development over the course of the text, including its relationship to supporting ideas; providing an objective summary of the text

Title of text:

RI 9.2a–10.2a
Determining a central idea of a text and analyzing its development over the course of the text, including how it emerges and is shaped and refined by specific details;
providing an objective summary of the text

Title of text:	Central idea:

Key details that support the development of the central idea:

Key detail 1:	Check one: ☐ Emergent ☐ Shaping ☐ Refining
Key detail 2:	Check one: ☐ Emergent ☐ Shaping ☐ Refining
Key detail 3:	Check one: ☐ Emergent ☐ Shaping ☐ Refining
Key detail 4:	Check one: ☐ Emergent ☐ Shaping ☐ Refining
Key detail 5:	Check one: ☐ Emergent ☐ Shaping ☐ Refining

EPIPHANY WORD BANK

Central Idea– the concept, thought, notion, or impression that is of greatest importance in the text or in a portion of the text; it may be implied or explicitly stated

Emergent– related to an introduction of an idea

Objective– not influenced by personal feelings or opinions in considering or representing facts

Shaping– related to providing more information on an idea, including establishing relevance/context

Summary– a brief statement that contains the essential ideas of a longer passage

Refine– to improve by making small changes

RI 9.2b–10.2b
Determining a central idea of a text and analyzing its development over the course of the text, including how it emerges and is shaped and refined by specific details; **provide an objective summary of the text**

Synthesize key details that support the central idea into a summary of the text. Be certain to include details that demonstrate the emergence, shaping, and refinement of the central idea.

RI 11.2a–12.2a

Determining two or more central ideas of a text and analyzing their development over the course of the text, including how they interact and build on one another to provide a complex analysis; providing an objective summary

Title of text:

Central idea 1:	Key detail that supports central idea 1:	Key detail that supports central idea 1:
Central idea 2:	Key detail that supports central idea 2:	Key detail that supports central idea 2:
Central idea 31:	Key detail that supports central idea 3:	Key detail that supports central idea 3:

© Educational Epiphany

EPIPHANY WORD BANK

Analysis– the process of separating material into its constituent elements or parts

Central Idea– the concept, thought, notion, or impression that is of greatest importance in the text or in a portion of the text; it may be implied or explicitly stated

Objective– not influenced by personal feelings or opinions in considering or representing facts including establishing relevance/context

Summary– a brief statement that contains the essential ideas of a longer passage

www.educationalepiphany.com | 410-258-6443

RI 11.2b–12.2b
Determining two or more central ideas of a text and analyzing their development over the course of the text, including how they interact and build on one another to provide a complex analysis; providing an objective summary

Title of text:

Central idea 1:	Central idea 2:

Key details that support the central idea 1:	Key details that support the central idea 2:

Explanation of how the central ideas **interact** over the course of the text to provide a complex analysis:	Explanation of how the central ideas **build upon one another** over the course of the text to provide a complex analysis:

RI 11.2c–12.2c

Determining two or more central ideas of a text and analyzing their development over the course of the text, including how they interact and build on one another to provide a complex analysis; providing an objective summary

Title of text:

Central idea 1:

Central idea 2:

Central idea 3:

Key details that support central idea 1:

Key details that support central idea 2:

Key details that support central idea 3:

Explanation of how the central ideas **interact** over the course of the text to provide a complex analysis:

Explanation of how the central ideas **build upon one another** over the course of the text to provide a complex analysis:

RI 11.2d–12.2d
Determining two or more central ideas of a text and analyzing their development over the course of the text, including how they interact and build on one another to provide a complex analysis; providing an objective summary

Synthesize the key details that support the two or more central ideas to objectively summarize the text.

Domain: Operations and Algebraic Thinking 3.OA.1

Cluster: Represent and solve problems involving multiplication and division.

Standard: Interpret products of whole numbers, e.g., interpret 5 × 7 as the total number of objects in 5 groups of 7 objects each.

For example, describe a context in which a total number of objects can be expressed as 5 × 7.

Given problem:	Given problem:	Given problem:
Interpret the product of whole numbers.	Interpret the product of whole numbers.	Interpret the product of whole numbers.
Describe a context for the problem.	Describe a context for the problem.	Describe a context for the problem.

EPIPHANY WORD BANK

Context– situation used to describe the mathematical problem

Describe– to represent in words using relevant details

Express– to state or share information

Group– to put together in the same category

Interpret– to make sense of and assign meaning to the data

Multiplication– repeated addition

Object– a material thing that can be seen or touched

Product– the result of a multiplication problem

Whole number– a number without fractions; an integer

© Educational Epiphany

www.educationalepiphany.com | 410-258-6443

Domain: Operations and Algebraic Thinking 3.OA.2

Cluster: Represent and solve problems involving multiplication and division.

Standard: Interpret whole-number quotients of whole numbers, e.g., interpret 56 ÷ 8 as the number of objects in each share when 56 objects are partitioned equally into 8 shares, or as a number of shares when 56 objects are partitioned into equal shares of 8 objects each.

For example, describe a context in which a number shares or a number of groups can be expressed as 56 ÷ 8.

Given problem:	Given problem:	Given problem:
Interpret the quotient of whole numbers.	Interpret the quotient of whole numbers.	Interpret the quotient of whole numbers.
Describe a context for the problem.	Describe a context for the problem.	Describe a context for the problem.

EPIPHANY WORD BANK

Context– situation used to describe the mathematical problem

Describe– to represent in words using relevant details

Division– repeated subtraction

Equal– exactly the same amount or value

Express– to state or share information

Group– to put together in the same category

Interpret– to make sense of and assign meaning to the data

Object– a material thing that can be seen or touched

Partitioned– divided

Quotient– the answer after you divide one number by another

Share– to split into equal parts or groups

Whole number– a number without fractions; an integer

www.educationalepiphany.com | 410-258-6443

Domain: Operations and Algebraic Thinking 3.OA.3

Cluster: Represent and solve problems involving multiplication and division.

Standard: Use multiplication and division within 100 to solve word problems in situations involving equal groups, arrays, and measurement quantities, e.g., by using drawings and equations with a symbol for the unknown number to represent the problem.

Word problem involving equal groups, arrays, and measurement quantities:	Equation:
	(if applicable)
Interpret the product of whole numbers.	Solution:
	(Show work)

EPIPHANY WORD BANK

Array– items (such as objects, numbers, etc.) arranged in rows and columns

Diagram– a drawing used to describe something

Division– repeated subtraction

Equal– exactly the same amount or value

Group– to put together in the same category

Multiplication– repeated addition

Represent– to explain, show or model

Symbol– a pattern or image used instead of words

Unknown– not known; missing

© Educational Epiphany

www.educationalepiphany.com | 410-258-6443

Domain: Operations and Algebraic Thinking 3.OA.4

Cluster: Represent and solve problems involving multiplication and division.

Standard: Determine the unknown whole number in a multiplication or division equation relating three whole numbers.

For example, determine the unknown number that makes the equation true in each of the equations 8 × ? = 48, 5 = □ ÷ × 3, 6 × 6 = ?

Equation:

Determine the unknown.

Equation:

Determine the unknown.

Equation:

Determine the unknown.

Equation:

Determine the unknown.

Equation:

Determine the unknown.

EPIPHANY WORD BANK

Determine– to find out something by using mathematical processes

Division– repeated subtraction

Equation– a mathematical statement that assigns equivalence

Multiplication– repeated addition

Relate– to show or make a connection between (two or more things)

Unknown– not known; missing

Whole number– a number without fractions; an integer

Domain: Operations and Algebraic Thinking 3.OA.5 (Commutative Property)

Cluster: Understand properties of multiplication and the relationship between multiplication and division.

Standard: Apply properties of operations as strategies to multiply and divide. *Examples: If 6 × 4 = 24 is known, then 4 × 6 = 24 is also known. (Commutative property of multiplication) 3 × 5 × 2 can be found by 3 × 5 = 15, then 15 × 2 = 30, or by 5 × 2 = 10, then 3 × 10 = 30. (Associative property of multiplication) Knowing that 8 × 5 = 40 and 8 × 2 = 16, one can find 8 × 7 as 8 × (5 + 2) = (8 × 5) + (8 × 2) = 40 + 16 = 56. (Distributive property)*

Equation:

Apply the commutative property of multiplication.

Equation:

Apply the commutative property of multiplication.

EPIPHANY WORD BANK

Array– items (such as objects, numbers, etc.) arranged in rows and columns

Diagram– a drawing used to describe something

Division– repeated subtraction

Equal– exactly the same amount or value

Group– to put together in the same category

Multiplication– repeated addition

Represent– to explain, show or model

Symbol– a pattern or image used instead of words

Unknown– not known; missing

Commutative property of multiplication– When two numbers are multiplied together, the product is the same regardless of the order of the numbers.

$a × b = b × a$

Example: $4 × 2 = 2 × 4$

Associative property of multiplication– When three or more numbers are multiplied, the product is the same regardless of the grouping of the numbers.

$(a × b) × c = a × (b × c)$

Example: $(2 × 3) × 4 = 2 × (3 × 4)$

Distributive property of multiplication– The sum of two numbers times a third number is equal to the sum of each addend times the third number.

$a (b + c) = (a × b) + (a × c)$

Example: $4 (6 + 3) = (4 × 6) + (4 × 3)$

Domain: Operations and Algebraic Thinking 3.OA.5 (Associative Property)

Cluster: Understand properties of multiplication and the relationship between multiplication and division.

Standard: Apply properties of operations as strategies to multiply and divide. *Examples: If 6 × 4 = 24 is known, then 4 × 6 = 24 is also known. (Commutative property of multiplication) 3 × 5 × 2 can be found by 3 × 5 = 15, then 15 × 2 = 30, or by 5 × 2 = 10, then 3 × 10 = 30. (Associative property of multiplication) Knowing that 8 × 5 = 40 and 8 × 2 = 16, one can find 8 × 7 as 8 × (5 + 2) = (8 × 5) + (8 × 2) = 40 + 16 = 56. (Distributive property)*

Equation:

Apply the associative property of multiplication.

Commutative property of multiplication– When two numbers are multiplied together, the product is the same regardless of the order of the numbers. $a \times b = b \times a$ Example: $4 \times 2 = 2 \times 4$

Equation:

Apply the associative property of multiplication.

Associative property of multiplication– When three or more numbers are multiplied, the product is the same regardless of the grouping of the numbers. $(a \times b) \times c = a \times (b \times c)$ Example: $(2 \times 3) \times 4 = 2 \times (3 \times 4)$

Distributive property of multiplication– The sum of two numbers times a third number is equal to the sum of each addend times the third number. $a (b + c) = (a \times b) + (a \times c)$ Example: $4 (6 + 3) = (4 \times 6) + (4 \times 3)$

EPIPHANY WORD BANK

Determine– to find out something by using mathematical processes

Division– repeated subtraction

Equation– a mathematical statement that assigns equivalence

Multiplication– repeated addition

Relate– to show or make a connection between (two or more things)

Unknown– not known; missing

Whole number– a number without fractions; an integer

Domain: Operations and Algebraic Thinking 3.OA.5 (Distributive Property)

Cluster: Understand properties of multiplication and the relationship between multiplication and division.

Standard: Apply properties of operations as strategies to multiply and divide. *Examples: If 6 × 4 = 24 is known, then 4 × 6 = 24 is also known. (Commutative property of multiplication.) 3 × 5 × 2 can be found by 3 × 5 = 15, then 15 × 2 = 30, or by 5 × 2 = 10, then 3 × 10 = 30. (Associative property of multiplication.) Knowing that 8 × 5 = 40 and 8 × 2 = 16, one can find 8 × 7 as 8 × (5 + 2) = (8 × 5) + (8 × 2) = 40 + 16 = 56. (Distributive property)*

Equation:	Apply the distributive property of multiplication.
Equation:	Apply the distributive property of multiplication.

Commutative property of multiplication– When two numbers are multiplied together, the product is the same regardless of the order of the numbers.

a × b = b × a

Example: 4 × 2 = 2 × 4

Associative property of multiplication– When three or more numbers are multiplied, the product is the same regardless of the grouping of the numbers.

(a × b) x c = a × (b × c)

Example: (2 × 3) × 4 = 2 × (3 × 4)

Distributive property of multiplication– The sum of two numbers times a third number is equal to the sum of each addend times the third number.

a (b + c) = (a × b) + (a × c)

Example: 4 (6 + 3) = (4 × 6) + (4 × 3)

EPIPHANY WORD BANK

Determine– to find out something by using mathematical processes

Division– repeated subtraction

Equation– a mathematical statement that assigns equivalence

Multiplication– repeated addition

Relate– to show or make a connection between (two or more things)

Unknown– not known; missing

Whole number– a number without fractions; an integer

www.educationalepiphany.com | 410-258-6443

Domain: Operations and Algebraic Thinking 3.OA.6

Cluster: Understand properties of multiplication and the relationship between multiplication and division.

Standard: Understand division as an unknown-factor problem. *For example, find 32 ÷ 8 by finding the number that makes 32 when multiplied by 8.*

Given division problem:	Write a multiplication number sentence that represents the division problem.
Given division problem:	Write a multiplication number sentence that represents the division problem.
Given division problem:	Write a multiplication number sentence that represents the division problem.

EPIPHANY WORD BANK

Division– repeated subtraction

Fact– an addition/subtraction or multiplication/division number sentence

Factor– a whole number that multiplies with another number to make a third number

Multiplication– repeated addition

Unknown– not known, missing

© Educational Epiphany

www.educationalepiphany.com | 410-258-6443

205

Domain: Operations and Algebraic Thinking 3.OA.7a

Cluster: Multiply and divide within 100.

Standard: Fluently multiply and divide within 100, using strategies such as the relationship between multiplication and division (e.g., knowing that 8 × 5 = 40, one knows 40 ÷ 5 = 8) or properties of operations. By the end of Grade 3, know from memory all products of two one-digit numbers.

Given problem:

Solve the problem using multiplication or division.

(Show work using a strategy).

Given problem:

Solve the problem using multiplication or division.

(Show work using a strategy).

EPIPHANY WORD BANK

Digit– any of the numerals from 0 to 9

Divide– to split into equal parts or groups

Fluently– readily able to speak or write

Multiply– repeated addition

Operation– a mathematical process

Product– result of a multiplication problem

Property– a mathematical rule

Relationship– the way in which two or more concepts are connected

Strategy– a method or way of solving a problem

Domain: Operations and Algebraic Thinking 3.OA.7b

Cluster: Multiply and divide within 100.

Standard: Fluently multiply and divide within 100, using strategies such as the relationship between multiplication and division (e.g., knowing that 8 × 5 = 40, one knows 40 ÷ 5 = 8) or properties of operations. By the end of Grade 3, know from memory all products of two one-digit numbers.

	0	1	2	3	4	5	6	7	8	9	10
0											
1											
2											
3											
4											
5											
6											
7											
8											
9											
10											

EPIPHANY WORD BANK

Digit– any of the numerals from 0 to 9
Divide– repeated subtraction
Fluently– readily able to speak or write
Multiply– repeated addition
Operation– a mathematical process

Product– result of a multiplication problem
Property– a mathematical rule
Relationship– the way in which two or more concepts are connected
Strategy– a method or way of solving a problem

www.educationalepiphany.com | 410-258-6443

Domain: Operations and Algebraic Thinking 3.OA.8

Cluster: Solve problems involving the four operations, and identify and explain patterns in arithmetic.

Standard: Solve two-step word problems using the four operations. Represent these problems using equations with a letter standing for the unknown quantity. Assess the reasonableness of answers using mental computation and estimation strategies including rounding.

Two-step word problem:

Representation of problem using an equation.

Describe the reasonableness of the problem using mental computation and estimation strategies.

Rounding Rules

1. Locate the rounding digit.

2. If the digit to the right of the rounding digit is 0, 1, 2, 3, or 4 do NOT change the rounding digit. All other digits to the right become zero.

3. If the digit to the right of the rounding digit is 5, 6, 7, 8, or 9 increase the rounding digit by one. All other digits to the right become zero

Examples

Tens:		
2̲8	30	
	2̲1	20
Hundreds:		
5̲87	600	
	5̲02	500
Thousands:		
3̲,902	4,000	
	3̲,3418	3,000

EPIPHANY WORD BANK

Assess– evaluate

Equation– a mathematical statement that assigns equivalence

Estimate– an approximate value

Mental Computation– mental processes used to achieve the answer

Operation– a mathematical process

Quantity– how much there is of something

Represent– to explain, show or model

Reasonable– logical

Rounding– to replace a number with an approximation

Solve– to find the answer

Unknown– not known, missing

www.educationalepiphany.com | 410-258-6443

Domain: Operations and Algebraic Thinking 3.OA.9

Cluster: Solve problems involving the four operations, and identify and explain patterns in arithmetic.

Standard: Identify arithmetic patterns (including patterns in the addition table or multiplication table), and explain them using properties of operations. *For example, observe that 4 times a number is always even, and explain why 4 times a number can be decomposed into two equal addends.*

0	1	2	3	4	5	6	7	8	9	10
0										
1										
2										
3										
4										
5										
6										
7										
8										
9										
10										

Given arithmetic pattern.

Explain the arithmetic pattern using properties of operations.

Identify the increments that the number pattern is increasing or decreasing.

EPIPHANY WORD BANK

Arithmetic pattern– pattern of numbers that has a constant difference between every two consecutive terms

Describe– represent in words using relevant details

Explain– make clear by describing

Identify– recognize and name

Increment– the amount by which something increases or grows

Operation– a mathematical process

Property– a mathematical rule

© Educational Epiphany

www.educationalepiphany.com | 410-258-6443

209

Domain: Number and Operations in Base Ten 5.NBT.1

Cluster: Understand the place value system

Standard: Recognize that in a multi-digit number, a digit in one place represents 10 times as much as it represents in the place to its right and $\frac{1}{10}$ of what it represents in the place to its left.

Multi-digit number		Value of the digit one place to the right of identified digit.	Value of the digit one place to the left of identified digit.
	Select a place value.		
Multi-digit number		Value of the digit one place to the right of identified digit.	Value of the digit one place to the left of identified digit.
	Select a place value.		
Multi-digit number		Value of the digit one place to the right of identified digit.	Value of the digit one place to the left of identified digit.
	Select a place value.		

Digit– any of the numerals from 0 to 9

Multi– more than one; many

One-tenth– one part in ten equal parts

EPIPHANY WORD BANK

Represent– to explain show or model

Ten times– equal to or having 10 times as many or as much

Domain: Number and Operations in Base Ten 5.NBT.2a (Number)

Cluster: Understand the place value system

Standard: Explain patterns in the number of zeros of the product when multiplying a number by powers of 10, and explain patterns in the placement of the decimal point when a decimal is multiplied or divided by a power of 10. Use whole-number exponents to denote powers of 10.

Given problem:

Explain the pattern of zeros in the product.

Be sure to use whole-number exponents to denote powers of 10.

Given problem:

Explain the pattern of zeros in the product.

Be sure to use whole-number exponents to denote powers of 10.

EPIPHANY WORD BANK

Decimal point– a point or dot used to separate the whole number part from the fractional part of a number

Denote– indicate

Divide– to split into equal parts or groups

Explain– make clear by describing

Exponent– used to show the number of times the base number is multiplied by itself

Multiply– repeated addition

Pattern– repeated/recurring outcome

Power– how many times a number is multiplied by itself

Product– the result of a multiplication problem

www.educationalepiphany.com | 410-258-6443

Domain: Number and Operations in Base Ten 5.NBT.2b (Decimal)

Cluster: Understand the place value system

Standard: Explain patterns in the number of zeros of the product when multiplying a number by powers of 10, and explain patterns in the placement of the decimal point when a decimal is multiplied or divided by a power of 10. Use whole-number exponents to denote powers of 10.

Given problem:

Explain the pattern in the placement of the decimal point in your answer.

Given problem:

Explain the pattern in the placement of the decimal point in your answer.

EPIPHANY WORD BANK

Decimal Point– a point or dot used to separate the whole number part from the fractional part of a number

Denote– indicate

Divide– to split into equal parts or groups

Explain– make clear by describing

Exponent– used to show the number of times the base number is multiplied by itself

Multiply– repeated addition

Pattern– repeated/recurring outcome

Power– how many times a number is multiplied by itself

Product– the result of a multiplication problem

www.educationalepiphany.com | 410-258-6443

Domain: Number and Operations in Base Ten 5.NBT.3a

Cluster: Understand the place value system

Standard: Read and write decimals to the thousandths using base-ten numerals, number names, and expanded form,

e.g., 347.392 = 3 × 100 + 4 × 10 + 7 × 1 + 3 × ($\frac{1}{10}$) + 9 × ($\frac{1}{100}$) + 2 × ($\frac{1}{1000}$).

Decimal to be read or written:

Decimal to be read or written:

Decimal to be read or written:

EPIPHANY WORD BANK

Base-ten numeral- a number written using place value

Decimal– a fraction whose denominator is a power of ten and whose numerator is expressed by figures placed to the right of a decimal point

Expanded form– a way to write a number that shows the sum of values of each digit of a number

Number name– word name of a number, e.g., 2 is two

Thousandth– being one of a thousand equal parts

Domain: Number and Operations in Base Ten 5.NBT.3b

Cluster: Understand the place value system

Standard: Compare two decimals to thousandths based on meanings of the digits in each place, using >, =, and < symbols to record the results of comparisons.

Relational Symbols
> Greater than
< Less than
= Equal to

Compare given decimals.

Compare given decimals.

Compare given decimals.

Compare given decimals.

Compare– to relate two numbers to each other

Decimal– a fraction whose denominator is a power of ten and whose numerator is expressed by figures placed to the right of the decimal point

Digit– any of the numerals from 0 to 9

Symbol– a pattern or image used instead of words

Thousandth– being one of a thousand equal parts

Domain: Number and Operations in Base Ten 5.NBT.4

Cluster: Understand the place value system

Standard: Use place value understanding to round decimals to any place.

Round the given decimal.

_____

starting decimal

Round the given decimal.

_____

starting decimal

Round the given decimal.

_____

starting decimal

_____

starting decimal

_____

starting decimal

_____

starting decimal

Rounding Rules

1. Locate the rounding digit.

2. If the digit to the right of the rounding digit is 0, 1, 2, 3, or 4 do NOT change the rounding digit. All other digits to the right become zero.

3. If the digit to the right of the rounding digit is 5, 6, 7, 8, or 9 increase the rounding digit by one. All other digits to the right become zero.

Domain: Number and Operations in Base Ten 5.NBT.5

Cluster: Perform operations with multi-digit whole numbers and with decimals to hundredths.

Standard: Fluently multiply multi-digit whole numbers using the standard algorithm.

Solve the given multiplication problem.

Answer:

Solve the given multiplication problem.

Answer:

Solve the given multiplication problem.

Answer:

Algorithm– a step by step solution to a problem

Digit– any of the numerals from 0 to 9

Fluently– easily

Multi– more than one; many

EPIPHANY WORD BANK

Multiply– repeated addition

Standard– common; model

Whole number– a number without fractions; an integer

Domain: Number and Operations in Base Ten 5.NBT.6

Cluster: Perform operations with multi-digit whole numbers and with decimals to hundredths.

Standard: Find whole-number quotients of whole numbers with up to four-digit dividends and two-digit divisors, using strategies based on place value, the properties of operations, and/or the relationship between multiplication and division. Illustrate and explain the calculation by using equations, rectangular arrays, and/or area models.

Solve the given division problem (with four-digit dividends and two-digit divisions):

Answer:

Explain the calculation by using equations.

Illustrate the calculation by using a rectangular array.

Illustrate the calculation by using an area model.

EPIPHANY WORD BANK

Area model– a model for math problems, where the length and width are configured using either multiplication, percentage or fractions to figure out the size

Digit– any of the numerals from 0 to 9

Divide– repeated subtraction

Dividend– the number being divided

Divisor– a number that divides the dividend

Equation– a mathematical statement that assigns equivalence

Multiply– repeated addition

Operation– a mathematical process

Place value– the numerical value that a digit has by virtue of its position in a number

Property– a character or attribute that some thing has

Quotient– the result of a division problem

Rectangular array– rectangular arrangement of quantities in rows and columns

Whole Number– a number without a fraction; an integer

Domain: Number and Operations in Base Ten 5.NBT.7

Cluster: Perform operations with multi-digit whole numbers and with decimals to hundredths.

Standard: Add, subtract, multiply, and divide decimals to hundredths, using concrete models or drawings and strategies based on place value, properties of operations, and/or the relationship between addition and subtraction; relate the strategy to a written method and explain the reasoning used.

Solve the given decimals problem using a model, drawing, or strategy.

Relate the strategy used above to a written method and explain the reasoning used.

EPIPHANY WORD BANK

Add– to join to something so as to increase the number

Concrete model– meaningful example

Decimal– a fraction whose denominator is a power of ten and whose numerator is expressed by figures placed to the right of a decimal point

Divide– repeated subtraction

Drawing– a picture or diagram made with a pencil, pen, or crayon rather than paint

Hundredth– being one of hundred equal parts

Multiply– repeated addition

Operation– a mathematical process

Place value– the numerical value that a digit has by virtue of its position in a number

Relationship– the way in which two or more concepts are connected

Strategy– a method or way of solving a problem

Domain: Statistics and Probability 7.SP.1

Cluster: Use random sampling to draw inferences about a population.

Standard: Understand that statistics can be used to gain information about a population by examining a sample of the population; generalizations about a population from a sample are valid only if the sample is representative of the population; understand that random sampling tends to produce representative samples and support valid inferences.

Describe the larger population.	Describe a random sample of the larger population.

Statistic(s) about the random sample.	Make a generalization about the larger population from the random sample.

Explain the relationship between generalizations and the representative sample. What makes the generalization a valid inference?

EPIPHANY WORD BANK

Examine— look at something carefully in order to learn more about it

Generalization– inferring the results from a sample and applying it to a population

Inference– the process of drawing conclusions from data

Population– the whole group from which a sample is taken

Random–without order; not able to be predicted; happening by chance

Relationship– the way in which two or more concepts are connected

Representative– typical of a class, group, or body of opinion

Sample–a selection taken from a larger group (the "population")

Statistics– the study of data: how to collect, summarize and present it

Subset– a set that is part of a larger set

Valid– relevant and logical

Domain: Statistics and Probability 7.SP.2

Cluster: Use random sampling to draw inferences about a population.

Standard: Use data from a random sample to draw inferences about a population with an unknown characteristic of interest; generate multiple samples (or simulated samples) of the same size to gauge the variation in estimates or predictions.

Identify a random sample.

Draw inferences about the population with an unknown characteristic of interest.

Generate a sample of the same size.

Generate a sample of the same size.

Generate a sample of the same size.

Interpret the variation in estimates or predictions in the simulated samples.

EPIPHANY WORD BANK

Characteristic– a feature belonging to a population

Generate– to produce

Inference– the process of drawing conclusions from data

Population– the whole group from which a sample is taken

Random–without order; not able to be predicted; happening by chance

Relationship– the way in which two or more concepts are connected

Representative– small quantity of a larger population

Sample– a selection taken from a larger group (the "population")

Simulate– imitate

Statistics– the study of data: how to collect, summarize and present it

Unknown– not known

Variation– how far a set of numbers is spread out

© Educational Epiphany

www.educationalepiphany.com | 410-258-6443

Domain: Statistics and Probability 7.SP.3

Cluster: Draw informal comparative inferences about two populations.

Standard: Informally assess the degree of visual overlap of two numerical data distributions with similar variabilities, measuring the difference between the centers by expressing it as a multiple of a measure of variability.

Data set 1:

Data set 2:

Display numerical data from data set 1 using graphs.

Determine the mean for data set 1.

Display numerical data from data set 2 using graphs.

Determine the mean for data set 2.

Measure the difference between the centers using multiple measures of variability.

EPIPHANY WORD BANK

Assess– evaluate

Data– a collection of facts, such as values or measurements

Difference– the result of subtracting one number from another. How much one number differs from another .

Measure– to find a number that shows the size or amount of something

Similar– having like characteristics

Variability– the measure of how spread out statistical data may be

Domain: Statistics and Probability 7.SP.4

Cluster: Draw informal comparative inferences about two populations.

Standard: Use measures of center and measures of variability for numerical data from random samples to draw informal comparative inferences about two populations.

Population 1:	Population 2:
Random sample data set 1:	Random sample data set 2:
Calculate the measure of center and the measure of variability for random sample data set 1:	Calculate the measure of center and the measure of variability for random sample data set 2:
Determine informal inferences about population 1.	Determine informal inferences about population 2.

EPIPHANY WORD BANK

Comparative– involving the act of looking at the ways that things are alike or different

Data– a collection of facts, such as values or measurements

Inference– the process of drawing conclusions from data

Mean– is the average of the numbers

Measure of Center– a number which summarizes all the values in a set of dat

Measure of Variability– the spread of data

Population–the whole group from which a sample is taken

Random–without order; not able to be predicted; happening by chance

Range– the difference between the lowest and highest values

Sample–a selection taken from a larger group (the "population")

Variance–how far a set of numbers is spread out

Domain: Statistics and Probability 7.SP5

Cluster: Investigate chance processes and develop, use, and evaluate probability models.

Standard: Understand that the probability of a chance event is a number between 0 and 1 that expresses the likelihood of the event occurring; larger numbers indicate greater likelihood; a probability near 0 indicates an unlikely event, a probability around $\frac{1}{2}$ indicates an event that is neither unlikely nor likely, and a probability near 1 indicates a likely event.

Describe a chance event.	Calculate the probability of the event occurring.
	Describe valid conclusions about the probability of the event.
Describe a chance event.	Calculate the probability of the event occurring.
	Describe valid conclusions about the probability of the event.

EPIPHANY WORD BANK

Chance Event– the likelihood than a certain event will occur

Likelihood– the probable chances that a certain event will occur

Probability– the chance an event will occur

Domain: Statistics and Probability 7.SP6

Cluster: Investigate chance processes and develop, use, and evaluate probability models.

Standard: Approximate the probability of a chance event by collecting data on the chance process that produces it and observing its long-run relative frequency, and predict the approximate relative frequency given the probability.

Approximate the probability of a chance event.	Approximate the probability of a chance event.	Approximate the probability of a chance event.
Predict the approximate relative frequency.	Predict the approximate relative frequency.	Predict the approximate relative frequency.

EPIPHANY WORD BANK

Approximate– not exact, but close enough to be used

Chance Event– the likelihood that a certain event will occur

Chance Process– the likelihood that a certain process will occur

Data– a collection of facts, such as values or measurements

Frequency– how often something happens (usually during a period of time)

Predict– to tell what you think will occur

Probability– the chance an event will occur

Relative Frequency– is the observed number of successful events for a sample of trials

www.educationalepiphany.com | 410-258-6443

Domain: Statistics and Probability 7.SP.7.a

Cluster: Develop a uniform probability model by assigning equal probability to all outcomes, and use the model to determine probabilities of events.

Standard: Investigate chance processes and develop, use, and evaluate probability models.

Develop a uniform probability model with equal probability for all outcomes.	Determine probabilities of events using the model.
Develop a uniform probability model with equal probability for all outcomes.	Determine probabilities of events using the model.

© Educational Epiphany

EPIPHANY WORD BANK

Develop– to create

Equal–to have the same quantity

Event– any of the possible outcomes of an experiment

Outcome– all possible results of a trial or an experiment

Model– to represent or show mathematical ideas and relationships using objects, pictures, graphs, equations, or other methods

Probability– the chance an event will occur

Uniform– identical or consistent

Domain: Statistics and Probability 7.SP.7.b

Cluster: Investigate chance processes and develop, use, and evaluate probability models.

Standard: Develop a probability model (which may not be uniform) by observing frequencies in data generated from a chance process.

Observation generated from a chance event:	Observation generated from a chance event:
Develop a probability model based on observations from a chance event.	Develop a probability model based on observations from a chance event.

EPIPHANY WORD BANK

Chance– the possibility that something will happen

Data– a collection of facts, such as values or measurements

Develop– to create

Frequency– how often something happens (usually during a period of time)

Generate– to produce

Model– to represent or show mathematical ideas and relationships using objects, pictures, graphs, equations, or other methods

Probability– the chance an event will occur

www.educationalepiphany.com | 410-258-6443

Domain: Statistics and Probability 7.SP.8.a

Cluster: Investigate chance processes and develop, use, and evaluate probability models.

Standard: Understand that, just as with simple events, the probability of a compound event is the fraction of outcomes in the sample space for which the compound event occurs.

Identify the simple event.	Identify the compound event.
Calculate the probability of the simple event.	Calculate the probability of the compound event.
Describe the probability of the simple event.	Describe the probability of the compound event.

EPIPHANY WORD BANK

Compound Event– the chance of two or more events happening

Fraction– part of a whole

Outcome– all possible results of a trial or experiment

Probability– the chance that an event will occur

Sample Space– an exhaustive list of all the possible outcomes of an experiment

Simple Event– the chance of one event happening

www.educationalepiphany.com | 410-258-6443

Domain: Statistics and Probability 7.SP.8.b

Cluster: Investigate chance processes and develop, use, and evaluate probability models.

Standard: Represent sample spaces for compound events using methods such as organized lists, tables and tree diagrams. For an event described in everyday language (e.g., "rolling double sixes"), identify the outcomes in the sample space which compose the event.

Compound event:

Identify the outcomes in the sample space representation using a list:

Identify the outcomes in the sample space representation using a table:

Identify the outcomes in the sample space representation using a tree-diagram:

EPIPHANY WORD BANK

Compound Event– the chance of two or more events happening

Event– any of the possible outcomes of an experiment

Identify– to recognize and name

List– a method for organizing data consecutively, typically one below another

Outcome– all possible results of a trial or experiment

Sample Space– an exhaustive list of all the possible outcomes of an experiment

Table– numbers or quantities arranged in rows and columns

Tree Diagram– used to display sample space by using one branch for each possible outcome

© Educational Epiphany

www.educationalepiphany.com | 410-258-6443

Domain: Statistics and Probability 7.SP.8.c

Cluster: Investigate chance processes and develop, use, and evaluate probability models.

Standard: Design and use a simulation to generate frequencies for compound events.

Given compound event:

Create sample space for compound event.
(i.e. list, table and/or tree diagram)

Design a simulation for the compound event.

Use the simulation to generate frequencies for the compound event.

EPIPHANY WORD BANK

Compound Event– the chance of two or more events happening

Design– to create

Frequency– how often something happens (usually during a period of time)

Generate– to produce

Identify– to recognize and name

Outcome– all possible results of a trial or experiment

Sample Space– an exhaustive list of all the possible outcomes of an experiment

Simulation– an approximate mathematical model designed to predict the outcome of an event(s)

www.educationalepiphany.com | 410-258-6443